Library Basics Series

1. *Learn Library of Congress Classification,* Helena Dittmann and Jane Hardy, 2000
2. *Learn Dewey Decimal Classification (Edition 21),* Mary Mortimer, 2000
3. *Learn Descriptive Cataloging,* Mary Mortimer, 2000
4. *Learn Library of Congress Subject Access,* Jacki Ganendran, 2000

Learn Library of Congress Subject Access

Jacki Ganendran

Library Basics, No. 4

The Scarecrow Press, Inc.
Lanham, Maryland, and London
in cooperation with
DocMatrix Pty Ltd, Canberra, Australia
2000

SCARECROW PRESS, INC.

Published in the United States of America
by Scarecrow Press, Inc.
4720 Boston Way, Lanham, Maryland 20706
www.scarecrowpress.com

4 Pleydell Gardens, Folkestone
Kent CT20 2DN, England

Design by Andrew Rankine Design Associates pty ltd, Canberra, Australia

British Library and National Library of Australia Cataloguing in Publication Information Available

Library of Congress Cataloging-in-Publication Data
Ganendran, Jacki.
   Learn Library of Congress subject access / Jacki Ganendran.
     p. cm. — (Library basics series ; no. 4)
   Includes bibliographical references (p.) and index.
   ISBN 0-8108-3695-5 (paper : alk. paper)
    1. Subject headings, Library of Congress. I. Title. II. Series.
Z695.Z8 L5237 2000
025.4'9—dc21   00-057381

CONTENTS

Introduction   4

1.   Introduction to Subject Cataloging   5

2.   Introduction to LCSH   18

3.   Assigning Subject Headings   26

4.   Subdivisions   31

5.   Pattern Headings and Multiple Subdivisions   40

6.   Names   47

7.   Subject Authority Files   56

8.   More Practice   64

Free-Floating Subdivisions   68

Pattern Headings   75

Answers   87

Glossary   100

Bibliography   105

Index   106

About the Author   107

INTRODUCTION

This book covers the skills necessary for a cataloger in a library or other information agency, whether at a professional or a paraprofessional level. It is suitable for use by students studying librarianship in universities, and others who are studying subject cataloging by themselves, with a specific goal, or as part of their continuing professional development. Since most catalogs provide some subject access, and the Library of Congress Subject Headings is the scheme most commonly used in libraries, it is important for all library students and most library staff to be familiar with at least the basics.

Throughout the book you will find exercises to practice and test your skills. There are answers for self-checking at the back of the book. You may not always agree completely with the answers given, and it is useful to check them with a teacher or experienced cataloger. Always bear in mind that there is often room for more than one interpretation or emphasis, particularly in the area of subject analysis.

References are made to the relevant section of the *Subject cataloging manual: subject headings* by way of the section numbers, e.g., H 1095 Free-Floating Subdivisions.

ACKNOWLEDGMENTS

I wish to thank Chris, Peta and Daniel for their patience, encouragement and support. Thanks also to Mary Mortimer for her continued support, and to my many students for their invaluable feedback.

Chapter 1
INTRODUCTION TO SUBJECT CATALOGING

Introduction

Cataloging is the preparation of bibliographic information for catalog records.

Catalogers use a set of cataloging tools, which are the agreed international rules and standards.

Cataloging consists of
- descriptive cataloging
- subject cataloging
- classification.

Subject Cataloging

Subject cataloging is the process of determining subject headings for an item. The cataloger seeks the headings which best represent the subjects of the work in words and/or phrases using an authoritative list.

Aims of Subject Cataloging

The aims of subject cataloging are
- to provide access by subject to all relevant materials
- to provide subject access to materials through all suitable principles of subject organization—i.e., matter, process, application
- to bring together all references to material on the same subject regardless of different terminology, different subject approaches, and the changing nature of the material itself
- to show affiliations among subject fields
- to provide entry at any level of analysis
- to provide entry through any vocabulary common to any considerable group of users
- to provide a formal description of the subject content of the item in the most precise terms possible, whether this be a word, phrase, class number, etc.
- to provide the means for the user to select from among all items in any particular category, e.g., most recent.

EXERCISE 1.1

1.   What is your understanding of a

     Subject:

Subject heading:

2. Write down as many subject headings lists as you can:

Who Uses Subject Headings Lists?

Subject headings lists are used by

- catalogers and indexers–to allocate headings
- searchers–to plan a search strategy–that is, to identify appropriate headings for use in searching for a particular topic. Searchers may be library users or library staff
- originators of documents (ideally) in order to use standard terminology.

EXERCISE 1.2

What needs do the following users have of a subject headings list?

1. Cataloger:

2. Reference adviser:

3. Library user:

4.   Acquisitions officer:

5.   Interlibrary loans officer:

6.   Author:

Vocabulary Control

The purpose of any list of subject headings or thesaurus is to control the terms used in a catalog, bibliography or index.

Controlled Vocabulary

A controlled vocabulary is one in which there is one term or notation for a concept.

It explicitly records the hierarchical and associative relations of a concept:
        e.g.,   Allergy
                Narrower term: Hay fever

It establishes the size or scope of each topic:
        e.g.,   Baseball
                Includes the concept of softball

It identifies synonymous terms and selects one preferred term:
        e.g.,   Capsicum
                Use: Peppers

For homonyms, it explicitly identifies the multiple concepts expressed by that word or phrase:
        e.g.,   Springs (mechanical devices)
                vs
                Springs (water sources)

Library of Congress subject headings (*LCSH*) is one example of a controlled list.

Thesaurus

A subject list which includes hierarchical relationships between headings is also called a thesaurus.

Uncontrolled Vocabulary

An uncontrolled vocabulary uses the actual words in a document as access points. Uncontrolled vocabulary is also referred to as natural language, or free text vocabulary.

Terms may be selected from the text or the title.

EXERCISE 1.3

1. List examples of systems that use

    Controlled vocabulary:

    Uncontrolled vocabulary:

2. What are the advantages and disadvantages of controlled and uncontrolled vocabulary?

    Controlled Vocabulary
    Advantages:

    Disadvantages:

    Uncontrolled Vocabulary
    Advantages:

Disadvantages:

Pre-Coordinate and Post-Coordinate Indexing
Pre-Coordination

In a pre-coordinate system, the parts of a heading are put together (pre-coordinated) by the cataloger or indexer to create a specific subject heading. Terms are put together in a specific pre-determined order.

To retrieve documents from the system, the searcher must use the same terms in the search strategy. This requires the searcher to put together the heading in the same form as constructed by the cataloger. There is no opportunity for the searcher to combine concepts in a search at the retrieval stage. (In some systems, search capabilities which allow each part of the subject heading to be accessed separately act in a "post-coordinate" way.)

> In *LCSH*, for example,
> Title   Standards for the lubrication of car wheels in the United States
> Heading   Car-wheels—Lubrication—United States

At the very least, the searcher needs to know what the subject heading begins with.

Post-Coordination

In a post-coordinate system, the cataloger may use several terms to cover all subjects.
The searcher can then search using Boolean operators (and, not, or) to construct the search.
The searcher need not be aware of all the terms used, and there is no order of terms involved.
> e.g., Title   Standards for the lubrication of car wheels in the United States
> Headings   Car wheels
> Lubrication
> United States
> Standards

The searcher will find this item by using any (or any combination) of the subject terms.

Synonyms
What is a synonym?

What tools could you use to identify synonyms?

EXERCISE 1.4

Provide synonyms for the following words or phrases:

Term	Synonym(s)
1. author	
2. stamp collecting	
3. car	
4. monograph	
5. trailer	
6. serial	
7. hiking	
8. saturated	
9. slack	
10. corpulence	
11. elevators	
12. hirsute	
13. shore	
14. rage	
15. hemp	

Homonyms

What is a homonym?

What tools could you use to identify homonyms?

EXERCISE 1.5

Provide two possible meanings for each of the following terms:

	Term		Meanings
1.	slack	1.	
		2.	
2.	slam	1.	
		2.	
3.	toast	1.	
		2.	
4.	lag	1.	
		2.	
5.	cuff	1.	
		2.	

Subject Analysis

Subject analysis involves several steps.

1. First, examine the work in hand.

2. Then decide on several keywords that could represent the subject.

3. Using the keywords as a starting point, go to each term in the list to identify appropriate headings.

EXERCISE 1.6

Comprehension and Summarizing

Choose the statement which best expresses the main idea of the following paragraphs. More than one answer in each group may be correct. You are not trying to find the correct answer but the best answer.

1. The writing of political comments on walls seems to me to be justified, then, as long as they contain messages that would not otherwise reach the people, and as long as the writers of these comments have no regular access to other media, such as newspapers or television. I only wish, though, that they would confine their aerosol activities to walls, and stop defacing public monuments and statues.

The writer approves of political graffiti only if they
a. attack the government
b. are written so that everyone can understand them
c. do not compete with the media (e.g., the press and television)
d. contain useful or important information.

2. Most of us lead unhealthy lives : we spend far too much time sitting down. If, in addition, we are careless about our diets, our bodies soon become flabby and our systems sluggish. Then the guilt feelings start: "I must go on a diet", "I must try to lose weight", "I must get more fresh air and exercise", "I must stop smoking", "I must try to keep fit". There are some aspects of our unhealthy lives that we cannot avoid. I am thinking of such features of modern urban life as pollution, noise, rushed meals and stress. But keeping fit is a way to minimize the effects of these evils.

Yoga, as practiced in the West, is the most widely known and popular of the systems for achieving the necessary state of relaxation. Contrary to popular belief, you do not have to learn a lot of strange words or become a Buddhist in order to benefit from Yoga. It seems ironical, though, that as our lives have improved in a material sense, we have found it increasingly necessary to go back to forms of activity –physical effort on the one hand, and relaxation on the other–which were the natural way of our forefathers.

i. Unfitness is the result of
   a. lack of fresh air and exercise
   b. overeating, smoking and living in towns
   c. not eating properly and not getting enough exercise
   d. not taking part in sports.

ii. Pollution, noise and stress are examples of
   a. causes of unfitness
   b. bad features of living in towns
   c. the things we must avoid if we are to stay healthy
   d. industrial life and work.

iii. Our reaction to being out of condition is to
   a. give up smoking and go on a diet
   b. start a program of keep-fit exercises
   c. make resolutions to lead a healthier life
   d. take up a sport.

iv. Many people believe that in order to practice yoga
   a. you must learn a special vocabulary
   b. it is better to become a Buddhist
   c. you must learn to relax completely
   d. you must wear special clothing.

v. Our forefathers were healthy because
   a. their way of life involved both exercise and relaxation
   b. they were careful to get plenty of fresh air and keep fit
   c. they lived in the country and spent time out of doors
   d. they had simple work to do and very little to worry about.

vi. List keywords that describe important concepts / ideas / points contained in the passage.

vii. Summarize the passage in one sentence.

Determining the Subject

The cataloger should examine the work in hand:

• Title	may or may not be helpful
• Subtitle	is often more useful
• Author	may provide an indication of the broad topic if the author has published in the area
• Foreword, preface, introduction	usually state the author's intention
• Publisher	may give an indication if the publisher specializes in a particular subject area
• Series	may be useful
• Contents and index	is usually a good indicator of the main topics
• Text	can be used to confirm your ideas about the subject
• Cataloging-in-publication	useful, but use with care, as CIPs are prepared prior to publication, often without the work in hand.

Example

When Your Partner Dies

Mary Mortimer

Hale & Iremonger

(title page)

Contents

	In Memoriam	6
	Acknowledgements	9
	Preface	11
	Introduction	15
1	Grief	19
2	Friends and family	31
3	Immediately	37
4	The funeral	43
5	Children	53
6	Food	59
7	Mail	61
8	Possessions	65
9	Fatigue	71
10	Helping to die	75
11	Will I ever be really happy again?	83
	Epilogue	85

Appendices:

A	Bereavement counselling services & helpful organisations	87
B	We all need laughter	89
C	Printed cards	90
D	Form letters	91
E	Funerals	92
F	Some useful books	93
G	Palliative care and hospice care	93
H	Taxation relief for donations	94
	Index	95

Preface

I have written this book in an attempt to make sense of the two major tragedies in my life–the deaths of two partners, each of whom I loved deeply. These deaths, and that of a dear friend, are my main personal experiences of bereavement. I have therefore focused on the death of a partner, although I am strongly aware of the devastation which can result from the death of a parent or a child.

When we lose a parent, and especially both parents, we lose the generation "above" us, the source of our life, our early knowledge of the world, so many of our characteristics and attitudes.

When our child dies, at whatever age, we are stunned by the unnatural order of events. We do not expect to survive our children: our hopes are for their future, even more than our own.

With the death of a partner, on the other hand, we lose the person who shares our everyday life, who is there for breakfast and dinner, with whom we share a home, a bed, many of our hopes and fears, memories and future plans. So the loss affects every aspect of our lives, and requires the most pervasive practical and emotional adjustments.

There are other books which present a more academic or professional approach to bereavement. I have written from my own experience–and that of close friends whose grief I have shared. I have been able to draw conclusions about the common aspects of grieving, and the different effects of sudden and of expected death. I try to offer practical suggestions for dealing with situations you may not yet have encountered.

Since I am a very practical person, and control over my life is of great importance to me, I emphasise what can be <u>done</u> in coping with the loss of a partner and its aftermath. You may find it easier than I did to let things happen, to accept this massive disruption to your physical and emotional life. I hope, however, that you will find my descriptions of events and feelings reassuring and helpful. One of our most valuable sources of support in times of crisis is the knowledge that our experience is not unique, and that others have felt or behaved in a similar way.

For most couples who are still together, one will have to live through and beyond the death of the other. Yet death is perhaps the last remaining taboo. Not only do we not talk about it, we don't even call it by name. We prefer to say that "the deceased" or the "dearly departed" or the "loved one" has "passed away", "gone", "left us", "gone to Heaven", is "at rest" or "at peace"; we talk around the event without using the words. By not naming death and dying, we deny the reality and make it more difficult for those who are close to it to share and express their sadness, their anxiety and their anger.

Many people who have no personal experience of death and loss, feel inadequate when a friend is bereaved. In their embarrassment they try to ignore this momentous event, and in so doing they add to their friend"s feelings of hurt and isolation.

If you believe in a God or gods, and a life after death, I am sure it can be a great source of comfort and strength. I hope you do not turn away from your belief in your anger and feeling of betrayal. "Why me?" is a very common reaction to tragedy. Though I do not believe in God or Heaven, I do have great faith in humankind: in our capacity to love and help each other, to share and give meaning to our joys and our sorrows. When I have felt most desolate, I have often asked "Why me?" Perhaps part of the answer lies in this book.

National Library of Australia Cataloguing-in-publication entry

Mortimer, Mary, 1944-

When your partner dies.

Bibliography.
ISBN 0 86806 417 3.
ISBN 0 86806 418 1 (pbk.)

1. Widowhood. 2. Bereavement. 3. Widows—Life skill guides.
4. Widowers—Life skill guides. I. Title

155.937 086 54

For *When your partner dies*, the technical examination provides this overview:

- Title   provides a lot of information. This book is clearly about what happens when a partner dies

- Subtitle   not applicable

- Author   not helpful

- Foreword, preface, introduction   preface explains the content and the author's intention

- Publisher   not helpful

- Series   not applicable

- Contents and index   contents confirm the subject of the work, including its practical nature

- Text   also confirms the subject

- Cataloging-in-publication   useful, though some headings are not in common use.

Principles of Subject Cataloging

User

The subject cataloger should always consider users and their needs. The heading, in wording and structure, should be one that the user will be most likely to look for.

Uniform Headings

All items dealing with one subject should be placed under one heading.

Terminology

The aim is always to match the user's term with the heading in the catalog. Several problems arise, since you must choose among
- synonyms
- variant spellings
- English vs other languages
- technical vs popular terms
- obsolete vs current terms
- homonyms.

Direct Entry

Ideally, identify a heading which directly describes the subject, e.g.,

    Cats

    not

    Mammals—Domestic animals—Cats

EXERCISE 1.7

Investigate the subject headings you would need to use to find information on the following topics.
Use two different types of libraries. Try to select two libraries which serve different clientele. Make a note if
you are unable to find any material on a topic in your library of choice. Why might this be?

Topic	Library 1	Library 2
1. National parks in Canada		
2. Building in tropical conditions		
3. Smoking and health		
4. Library classification schemes		
5. Fitting a jacket		
6. Women in business		
7. Desktop publishing		
8. Marketing your services		
9. The Second World War		
10. Cataloging non-book materials		
11. Presentation skills for new teachers		
12. Australian photographers		

Chapter 2
INTRODUCTION TO LIBRARY OF CONGRESS SUBJECT HEADINGS (LCSH)

Library of Congress subject headings (LCSH) is an accumulation of subject headings established by the Library of Congress since 1898. The *List of subject headings for use in dictionary catalogs*, prepared by a committee of the American Library Association and published in 1895, was the basis for the Library's own list of subject headings.

The first edition of the Library of Congress list was printed in parts between 1909 and 1914. The title changed to *Library of Congress subject headings* with the eighth edition in 1975.

Headings are created as needed when works are cataloged for the collections of the Library of Congress. Headings are also retained in new editions of the list, regardless of the recency or frequency of the list.

Inconsistencies in the formulation of headings can often be explained by the policies in force at the varying dates of their creation. *LCSH* is also an extremely large list, to which many individuals and groups of catalogers contribute.

Versions
Library of Congress subject headings are available in the following formats:
* Library of Congress subject headings–the printed version
* LCSH on fiche–the microfiche version.

Additional Publications
LCSH contains main headings, some subdivisions and references. Library of Congress policies and instructions on using *LCSH* are found in the *Subject cataloging manual: subject headings*. It is essential to use the Manual to ensure correct usage and to have access to additional subdivisions.

The following are also published by the Library of Congress, and contain information about changes:
* *Cataloging service bulletin*–a quarterly update of policy, headings and subdivisions
* *Free-floating subdivisions: an alphabetical index*–an annual index of all free-floating subdivisions
* *LC period subdivisions under names of places*
* *LC subject headings weekly lists*–new and revised headings, available on the Web (http://lcweb.loc.gov/catdir/cpso/) and on the Library of Congress gopher, LC MARVEL
* *Library of Congress subject headings: principles of structure and policies for application*–extracted from various LC documents.

Types of Headings Found in LCSH

The following types of headings are included:

Topical headings and subdivisions including types of objects and concepts
>   disciplines
>   methods and procedures
>   activities
>   industries
>   classes of people

Jurisdictional geographic names

Non-jurisdictional geographic names including geographic features
>   areas and regions
>   trails, parks and reserves
>   city sections
>   early cities, empires, kingdoms

Names of persons incapable of authorship and families including
>   legendary, mythological and fictitious characters
>   gods
>   dynasties
>   royal houses

Names of **art works**

Names of **chemicals, drugs and minerals;** biological names

Other proper names including
>   languages
>   computer languages and systems
>   ethnic groups
>   roads
>   structures and buildings
>   events
>   trade names
>   games.

Structure of Subject Headings (H 180)

Subject headings may take several forms:

- Single word–e.g., Dams
- Multiple words, direct heading–e.g., Data transmission systems
- Inverted heading–e.g., Art, Medieval
- Phrase heading–e.g., Photography of birds
- Complex phrase–e.g., Infants switched at birth
- Subdivided heading–e.g., Libraries–Government policy
- Qualified term–e.g., Seals (Animals)

Arrangement of LCSH

LCSH headings authorized for use as subject entries are printed in bold type in the printed version of *LCSH*. Authorized subdivisions are also printed in bold type.

The following symbols are used to codify the relationship between headings:

UF   Used For
BT   Broader Topic
RT   Related Topic
SA   See Also
NT   Narrower Topic
USE Use

(May Subd Geog)   Place names may follow the heading or subdivision.
(Not Subd Geog)   The Library of Congress has decided not to subdivide by place.

Headings without either designation have not yet been considered for geographic subdivision. They may not currently be subdivided by place. As headings are constantly reviewed, their status may change.

Scope notes are provided to ensure consistency of usage. A scope note
• specifies the range of subject matter to which a heading should be applied
• draws necessary distinctions between related headings
• states which of several meanings is the one to use.

EXERCISE 2.1

Study the following extract from *LCSH*, and answer the questions below.

Beverage containers   *(May Subd Geog)*
  BT Containers
  NT Advertising beverage containers
    Beer bottles
    Beer cans
    Carbonated beverage bottles
    Ginger beer bottles
    Liquor bottles
    Milk bottles
    Wine bottles
  —Law and legislation   *(May Subd Geog)*
  —Recycling
    UF Beverage container recycling
  ——Law and legislation
      (May Subd Geog)
      UF Beverage container deposit legislation
        Bottle bills
        Bottle law

Beverage industry *(May Subd Geog)*
    UF Drink industry
    RT Bottling
    NT Alcoholic beverage industry
        Brewing industry
        Coffee trade
        Distilling industries
        Fruit drink industry
        Fruit juice industry
        Mineral water industry
        Tea industry
        Soft drink industry
        Tea trade
    —Equipment and supplies
        NT Beverage processing machinery
Beverage managers, Hotel
    USE   Hotel beverage managers
Beverage processing machinery industry
    (May Subd Geog)
    BT Food processing plants
    NT Breweries
        Distilleries
        Milk plants
        Wineries
—Equipment and supplies
    NT Beverage processing machinery

1. Write down all authorized headings, ignoring the subdivisions. Do not include broader and narrower terms.

2. Write down all possible headings with subdivisions. Ignore geographic subdivisions.

3. Using **United States** as the place name, write down all possible headings with geographic subdivisions.

References (H 373)

LCSH contains cross-references that represent a mix of philosophies prevalent at different times in the history of the list. (This explains why cross-referencing practices are not consistent.)

USE (or SEE) References

USE references are made from **unauthorized** or **non-preferred** terms to an **authorized** or **preferred** heading. Under the preferred heading, there is a code UF which precedes the headings not used. For example,

> **Motor-cars**
> > USE Automobiles

> **Automobiles**
> > UF   Motor-cars

That is, **Automobiles** is the preferred term, and **Motor-cars** is the non-preferred term.

USE references are made from synonyms, variant spellings, variant forms of expression, alternate constructions of headings and older forms of headings. USE references may be used even when the heading and unused words are not synonymous.

Older catalogs may use the word SEE instead of USE.

References Indicating Hierarchical Relationships (H 370)

LCSH links subject headings in order to show the relationship between **broader** (**BT**) and **narrower** (**NT**) headings. This allows a user to make a search more general or more specific. The relationship is always reciprocal, e.g.,

>**Exterior lighting**
>>BT   Lighting

>**Lighting**
>>NT   Exterior lighting

A heading is normally linked to the one immediately next to it in the subject heading hierarchy (either immediately upward/broader or immediately lower/narrower).

The following relationships are considered hierarchical:

Genus/species
>**Apes**
>>BT Primates

Whole/part
>**Toes**
>>BT Foot

Instance (or generic topic/proper-named example):
>**Whitewater Lake (Wis.)**
>>BT Lakes—Wisconsin
>[Whitewater Lake is an instance of a lake in Wisconsin]

References Indicating Associated Relationships

LCSH also indicates relationships which are not broader or narrower but which are related. For example,

>**Ornithology**
>>RT   Birds

>**Birds**
>>RT   Ornithology

While there is no hierarchical relationship, terms are mentally associated to such an extent that the link reveals alternative headings that might be of interest.

General References (H371)

A general reference is made not to a specific heading but to an entire group of headings, frequently listing one or more headings as an example. This occurs because it is impractical to list all possible headings. For example,

Dog breeds
    SA   *names of specific breeds,* e.g., Bloodhounds, Collies

They can be made from a generic heading to a group of headings beginning with the same word, e.g.,

Chemistry
    SA   *headings beginning with the word* Chemical

Sometimes they lead to subdivisions, e.g.,

Economic history
    SA   *subdivision* Economic conditions *under names of countries, cities,* etc.

Sometimes general USE references can be made, e.g.,

Access control
    USE *subdivision* Access control *under subjects,* e.g., Computers—Access control; Psychiatry—Medical records—Access control

EXERCISE 2.2

Use this extract from *LCSH* to answer the questions below:

Artisans *(May Subd Geog)*
        UF   Artizans
                Craftsmen
        BT   Skilled labor
        RT   Cottage industries
        SA   *particular classes of artisans, e.g.,*
                Barbers; Cabinetmakers; Weavers
        NT   Apprentices
                Basket makers
                Diamond cutters

What is the relationship between

1.   Artisans and Craftsmen

2.   Artisans and Apprentices

3.   Artisans and Skilled labor

4.   Artisans and Cottage industries

5.   Is Craftsmen an authorized / permitted term?

EXERCISE 2.3
Use *LCSH* to determine if these are acceptable headings. If not, write down the correct term.

	Topic	Correct Heading
1.	Felix the Cat	
2.	Guitar—construction	
3.	Fusion reactors—Fuels	
4.	Fusion reactors—Germany	
5.	Semi-conductors	
6.	Guitar and harp music	
7.	Heliophobus plants	
8.	Seychelles—Coup d'etat, 1977	
9.	Coup d'etat—Seychelles	
10.	Tempo	

Chapter 3
ASSIGNING SUBJECT HEADINGS (H 180)

General Guidelines

General Rule
Assign one or more subject headings that best summarize the overall contents of the work. The aim is to provide access to the most important topics.

Specificity
Assign the most specific heading which represents exactly the contents of the work, e.g.,
> **Mathematics** and **Trigonometry** are not normally assigned to the same work.

Where a specific heading is not possible, assign a heading that is broader or more general than the topic.

Works on a Single Topic
Assign the one heading which represents exactly the contents of the work, e.g.,

Title	The world within the tide pool
Subject heading	**Tide pool ecology**

Subtopic Not Normally Subsumed under a Heading
Normally a work on a single topic can be expected to cover a range of subtopics. If, within such a work, there is a subtopic that falls outside the scope of the expected range, allocate headings for the main topic plus an additional heading for the subtopic. The subtopic should cover at least 20% of the work to warrant a separate heading, e.g.,

Title	Notes on planning and managing agricultural operations in Godavari
Subject headings	1. **Agriculture—India—Godavari—Statistics** 2. **Rice—India—Godavari**

Multi-Topic Works
For works on more than one topic treated separately, assign headings to bring out each concept individually, e.g.,

Title	Bibliography on snow, ice and frozen ground
Subject headings	1. **Snow—Bibliography** 2. **Ice—Bibliography** 3. **Frozen ground—Bibliography**

Hierarchical Considerations
(Topics which fit under a common theme)

Two or three related topics in a work
If a heading exists which represents precisely the two or three topics, assign it and not the two or three headings. For example,

Title	The distinctive excellences of Greek and Latin
Subject heading	**1. Classical literature**

(Separate headings are not used because Classical literature includes both Greek and Latin and nothing else.)

Rule of three
If a broad heading exists, but includes more than the two or three topics in question, assign the two or three headings, not the broader heading. For example,

Title	Travels in Brazil, Ecuador and Peru

Subject headings	**1. Brazil—Description and travel**
	2. Ecuador—Description and travel
	3. Peru—Description and travel
	(not the more inclusive South America)

Rule of four (four or more related topics in the work)
Do not assign a separate heading for each topic where a single heading which covers all topics can be used.

If no such heading exists, assign separate headings to four, or, if more than four, assign several very comprehensive headings or a single form heading. For example, a work on go-karts, hot rods, dragsters, sprint cars and Formula One cars should be assigned the heading **Automobiles, Racing.**

Multi-Element Works
If a work treats a single subject from different aspects or contains various elements of one topic, use one pre-coordinated heading, if there is one available. For example,

Title	Chemical plant management in the U.S.
Subject heading	**1. Chemical Plants—United States—Management**

However there are many subjects which are much more complex with no pre-coordinated heading available for use. In this case bring out each concept individually. For example,

Title	A method of setting up the eigenvalue problem for the linear, shallow-water wave equation for irregular bodies of water with variable water depth and application to bays and harbors in Hawaii.

Subject headings	**1. Ocean waves**
	2. Eigenvalues
	3. Oceanography—Data processing
	4. Bays—Hawaii
	5. Harbors—Hawaii

Principle Versus a Specific Case

If a work discusses a principle and illustrates the principle by referring to a specific case, assign a heading for the principle and also a heading for the specific case, if appropriate. For example, a work on the anatomy of vertebrates that illustrates this by reference to cats would get two subject headings, one for the main topic and one for the example.

Title	The anatomy of vertebrates
Subject headings	1. Vertebrates—Anatomy
	2. Cats

Additional Aspects
Place

If a work involves a specific geographic area, bring out the area by a subject heading or a subdivision.

Time

Express the chronological aspects significant to the contents of the work in situations where the Library of Congress subject heading system allows it.

Named Entities

Assign headings from the name authority file or subject authority file for individual persons, families, corporate bodies, projects, etc., that are significant to the content of the work.

Form

Assign form headings and subdivisions to represent what the item itself is—that is, its format or the particular type or arrangement of data that it contains—in situations where headings or subdivisions for these types of materials exist.

Viewpoint of Author or Publisher

Always consider this and assign a heading if useful. For example,

if the work is written primarily for a juvenile audience, use the subdivision
—Juvenile literature

If a general textbook is intended for specific persons, allocate a heading for the topic and one for the special interest or application. For example,

Title	Psychology for nurses
Subject headings	1. Psychology
	2. Nursing—Psychological aspects

Form Subject Headings

Form refers to the manner or style in which material is presented, the particular character or method of presentation of information, e.g., Aerial photographs, Biography, Catalogs and collections, Dictionaries and encyclopedias, Musical settings, Programmed learning.

Form can be designated by
• a topical subject heading with form subdivision
or
• a form subject heading.

Assign form subject headings to
• works produced in a particular format for "readers" with disabilities, e.g.,
  Large print books (often used for fiction in large print)
  Talking books (works reproduced on tape, disc or record for the visually impaired)

• rare books. If a work is held for its quality, uniqueness, or particular characteristics as a physical entity, a form subject to highlight this can be used, e.g.,
  Bibliography—Early printed books
  Bibliography—Fine editions
  Book ornamentation
  Bookbinding
  Chap-books
  Little press books

If a Subject Heading Is the Same as Another Access Point

Subject headings fulfill a different role from other access points–author, title, corporate body and so on. Therefore, subject headings should always be assigned to reflect the nature of the work and the subject being discussed.

EXERCISE 3.1

Using *LCSH*, provide a subject heading that best represents the following topics.

Topic	Subject Heading
1. The sea	
2. Adoption services	
3. Adriatic Islands	
4. Child actors	
5. Ways of monitoring fetal heart rate	
6. The impact of jet engine sounds	

7. Oceanic drilling ships in the Atlantic

_____

8. Catalan political satire

_____

9. An introduction to prehistoric agriculture

_____

10. The wonders of horseradish

_____

EXERCISE 3.2

Using *LCSH*, provide a subject heading that best represents the following topics.

Topic	Subject Heading
1. Morris West's slide collections	
2. Sleep-walking in literature	
3. Cartoon-makers	
4. Electric converters	
5. Music for harp and guitar	
6. Sulky racing	
7. Harmony on the keyboard	
8. Prehistoric cartography	
9. The benefits of asparaginic acid	
10. Bakery products	

Chapter 4
SUBDIVISIONS

Introduction

Subdivisions are used extensively in *LCSH*. They allow a number of different concepts to be combined in a single subject heading. Subdivisions serve two functions in *LCSH*:

- They make a subject more specific
- They may be used to sub-arrange a large number of items under one heading in a catalog.

Some subdivisions are printed in the list but these represent only a small fraction of possible combinations of headings and subdivisions. Others may be applied as instructed in the *Library of Congress subject cataloging manual.*

Authority to use subdivisions under a particular heading can be found in four places:

1. under the subject heading in its alphabetical place in the list

2. under the general subject heading which represents the subdivision you want

3. under the list of "Free-Floating Subdivisions" (this does not imply uncontrolled use)

4. under a "Pattern Heading".

Types of Subdivisions

There are four types of subdivisions–**topical, form, chronological** and **geographic**. Detailed instructions for assigning them appear in various sections of the Manual.

Topical Subdivisions

These are used to limit the concept expressed by the heading to a special subtopic, e.g.,

> Corn—Harvesting
> Automobiles—Motors—Carburetors

Form Subdivisions

These indicate the form in which the material on a subject is organized and presented. They are added as the last element in the string of terms. Form subdivisions can generally be used under any topic and are not usually listed. Most form subdivisions are indicated by a general *see also* reference under the heading representing the form as a whole, e.g.,

> Periodicals
> SA *subdivision* Periodicals *under subjects* e.g., Engineering—Periodicals.

Detailed guidance on the use of form subdivisions is given in the Manual.

Chronological or Period Subdivisions

These are used to limit a heading to a particular time period. These subdivisions may:

- denote chronological sequences under countries, e.g.,
Great Britain—History—George VI, 1936-1952

- mark significant dates in the evolution of a subject, e.g.,
Philosophy, French—18th Century

- divide a large file arbitrarily by date of publication, e.g.,
Mathematics—1961–
Aeronautics—Early works to 1800

Geographic Subdivisions

These may be added when the designation *(May Subd Geog)* appears after a heading or subdivision. The designation *(Not Subd Geog)* after a heading or subdivision indicates that the Library of Congress has made a decision not to subdivide by place. Headings without either designation may currently not be subdivided by place because they have yet to be reviewed to determine whether a geographic subdivision is possible or desirable.

EXERCISE 4.1

Using *LCSH*, allocate suitable subject headings to the following. Include one or more subdivisions to make your heading more specific.

Topic	Subject Heading
1. Economic conditions in Bologna	
2. Extensions to buildings	
3. Synthesis in organic chemistry	
4. Data processing in credit bureaus	
5. The rights and wages of employees in credit unions	
6. John Brown's raid on Harpers Ferry	
7. The 1929 depression in Chicago	
8. The diagnosis of unipolar depression	
9. Renaissance engraving	
10. Hunting with bows and arrows	

Free-Floating Subdivisions

The term "free-floating subdivision" refers to a form or topical subdivision that the cataloger may assign as required to particular subject headings.

- They may not be found in the printed listing or fiche.
- Sometimes they can be found under the subject heading they represent.
- They must be used in accordance with the guidelines in the Manual.

Example

Item   A monthly magazine for dentists

The item is about dentistry, so the main topic is Dentistry.
It is also a periodical.

Look at *LCSH* at the heading Periodicals, which provides the instruction
    SA   English [French etc.] periodicals;
           and subdivision Periodicals *under specific subjects, e.g.,*
           Engineering—Periodicals;
           United States—History—Periodicals.

So the subject heading is
           Dentistry—Periodicals.

Note that —Periodicals is a free-floating subdivision. A complete list of free-floating subdivisions can be found in section H 1095 in the Manual, along with instructions about their use. The list has been reproduced at the back of this book.

EXERCISE 4.2

Are the following subject headings and subdivisions correctly established? If not, why not?

Headings	Correct / Incorrect	Reason and Correct Form (if incorrect)
1. Dentistry—Law and legislation		
2. Paper industry—History		
3. Buildings—Maintenance		
4. Buildings—Maintenance and repair		
5. Books—Reviews—Periodicals		

6. Dentistry—Book reviews

_____ _____

7. Real property—Finance, personal

_____ _____

8. Chicago (Ill.)—Appropriations and expenditure

_____ _____

Geographic Subdivisions (H 830)

Below is listed an LC subject heading and some of its subdivisions as set out in *LCSH* 20th edition. If a heading contains both a geographic subdivision and a topical or form subdivision, the location of the geographic subdivision depends on which elements can be divided by place. Remember, if a geographic subdivision is allowable in two or more places in the sequence, choose the last.

LCSH Entry

Meat *(May Subd Geog)*
    BT   Animal products
           Food
    NT   Beef
           Canned meat
           Cookery (meat)
           and so on...
—Bacteriology
—Boning
—Labeling *(May Subd Geog)*
— —Law and legislation *(May Subd Geog)*
and so on.

Please note that this entry is not complete! See *LCSH* for the full list of headings.

Subject Headings Generated

    Meat
    Meat—Bacteriology
    Meat—United States—Bacteriology
    Meat—Boning
    Meat—United States—Boning
    Meat—Labeling
    Meat—Labeling—United States
    Meat—Labeling—Law and legislation
    Meat—Labeling—Law and legislation—United States
    Meat—Packaging
    Meat—United States—Packaging
    Meat—Packaging—Law and legislation—United States

EXERCISE 4.3

Here is an *LCSH* entry:

Banks and banking *(May Subd Geog)*
...
—Automation
——Equipment and supplies
—Branch banks
——Law and legislation *(May Subd Geog)*
...
—Government ownership *(May Subd Geog)*
——Law and legislation *(May Subd Geog)*

Write out all possible subdivisions, using **Canada** as a geographic subdivision.

E.g., Banks and banking—Canada

Indirect Geographic Subdivisions
General Rule
In many cases, the name of a larger geographic entity is placed before the name of a more specific locality. This is described as assigning the place name **indirectly**. Places below national level are normally assigned indirectly.

Generally, the name of the country is interposed between the topic and the subordinate political or geographic division, e.g.,

> Labor supply—France—Paris
> *instead of*
> Labor supply—Paris

> Litter (Trash)—Italy—Venice
> *instead of*
> Litter (Trash)—Venice

Exception
For places in the United States, Canada, and Great Britain, interpose the name of the first-order political division between the topic and the subordinate political or geographic division, e.g., Labor supply—California—Los Angeles
> *not*
> Labor supply—United States—Los Angeles

> Litter (Trash)—England—London
> *not*
> Litter (Trash)—Great Britain—London

As a general rule, place follows the last element that can be divided by place, e.g.,
> Construction industry *(May Subd Geog)*
> —Finance
> — —Law and legislation *(May Subd Geog))*
> —Government policy *(May Subd Geog)*
> —Industrial capacity

So the heading for a work on law and legislation in the construction industry in Indonesia is
> Construction industry—Finance—Law and legislation—Indonesia

Direct Geographic Subdivisions
If a geographic subdivision is at the country level or above, the name of the place follows the main heading or subdivision at the instruction *(May Subd Geog)*, e.g.,
> Futurism (Art)—France
> Health occupations students—Mexico
> Geology—Antarctica.

In addition, first order political divisions in
- Canada   provinces
- United States   states
- Great Britain   constituent countries (i.e., England, Wales, Scotland, Northern Ireland)
also follow the topical element directly.

So we have
Health occupations students—British Columbia
Geology—Australia—New South Wales.

EXERCISE 4.4

Using *LCSH*, allocate suitable subject headings to the following. Include one or more subdivisions to make your heading more specific.

	Topic	Subject Heading
1.	Diseases of the eyelids in China	
2.	Diseases of the forelimbs in Africa	
3.	Taxation of show business personalities in Australia	
4.	The labeling of bread in Houston	
5.	The legislation on bread labeling in Oregon	
6.	Abnormalities of cattle in Argentina	
7.	Collective agreements in the airlines in Belgium	
8.	Job stress in health professionals in Virginia	
9.	A report on potato pests in Victoria, Australia	
10.	Historical monuments in Mankato, Minnesota	

EXERCISE 4.5

Are these headings correct? If not, indicate a possible correct heading.

Topic	Subject Heading
1. Parachutes—Testing—Equipment—Certification—United States	
2. Scientific apparatus and instruments—Conservation and restoration	
3. United States—Climate—Measurement	
4. Birthparents—Identification—Case studies	
5. Chamber music—Early works to 1800—England	
6. Murderers—Civil rights—Boston (Mass.)	
7. Trade-unions—Accounting—Law and Legislation—Michigan	
8. Tuberculosis vaccines—Maine—Bangor	
9. Tuberculosis vaccines—Safety regulations—Maine—Bangor	
10. Separating machinery industry—Corrupt practices—London	

EXERCISE 4.6

Using *LCSH*, allocate suitable subject headings to the following. Include one or more subdivisions to make your heading more specific.

Topic	Subject Heading
1. Bibliography on plant migration	
2. Colonization of Zaire	

3. Pensions of bus drivers in Mexico   _____

4. History of the laws regulating collection
    agencies in Canada   _____

5. Satirical cartoons of nurses   _____

6. Laboratories for sensory evaluation in
    Geneva   _____

7. Diagnosis of mouth cancer in Glasgow   _____

8. Testing of instruments used in atomic
    absorption spectroscopy in Tokyo   _____

9. Deterioration of murals in Venice   _____

10. Care of clothing in the 19th century   _____

Chapter 5
PATTERN HEADINGS AND MULTIPLE SUBDIVISIONS

Introduction
Standardized sets of topical and form subdivisions have been developed for use under particular categories of subject headings or name headings. To avoid repeating these subdivisions under all possible subject headings, only one or a few representative headings from each category are printed in *LCSH*. These headings form patterns for other headings in their category. In this way they are a form of free-floating subdivision. The general free-floating subdivisions may not be included in all pattern headings.

You will also need to consult the Manual for the lists of free-floating subdivisions controlled by pattern headings (H 1147-H 1200) and other free-floating subdivisions if needed. Extracts from this section of the Manual can be found at the back of the book.

Subdivisions authorized for free-floating use have not generally been included in the lists of free-floating subdivisions controlled by pattern headings. It is frequently necessary to consult H 1095, H 1100, the list of free-floating subdivisions used under classes of persons and H 1105, the list of free-floating subdivisions used under corporate bodies, in addition to a specific pattern heading list when constructing subject headings with free-floating subdivisions.

Pattern headings have not been designated for all possible categories in the world of knowledge. Not all headings in *LCSH* are covered by pattern headings.

Procedure
1. Find the correct form of the main heading.
2. Check *LCSH* under the subject heading for the desired subdivision. If found, stop here.
3. If not found, check the list of free-floating subdivisions, or check for a free-floater as a heading.
4. If not found, check the list of Pattern Headings to find an appropriate category. Do not use a heading at the broader level (representing a class of items). You may need to check the list of free-floating subdivisions controlled by pattern headings as well.
5. Note: If two or more pattern headings are designated to represent a category, a subdivision established under any of these headings may be used as free-floating for a heading in that category if it is appropriate, and does not conflict with a heading established in the subject authority file in another form.
6. Once the correct pattern heading is located, use any of the subdivisions as required.

Pattern Headings Listed in Subject Cataloging Manual

Subdivisions Controlled by Pattern Headings   H 1146

List of pattern headings. Below and on the following pages is a chart showing pattern headings established to date. They are arranged first by major discipline, then by special category.

Subject Field	Category	Pattern Heading(s)	
RELIGION	Religious and monastic orders	Jesuits	H 1186
	Religions	Buddhism	H 1185
	Christian denominations	Catholic Church	H 1187
	Sacred works (including parts)	Bible	H 1188

Subject Field	Category	Pattern Heading(s)	
HISTORY AND GEOGRAPHY	Colonies of individual countries	Great Britain—Colonies	H 1149.5
	Legislative bodies (including individual chambers)	United States. Congress	H 1155
	Military services (including armies, navies, marines, etc.)	United States—Armed Forces	H 1159
		United States. Air Force	
		United States. Army	
		United States. Marine Corps	
		United States. Navy	
	Wars	World War, 1939-1945	H 1200
		United States—History —Civil War, 1861-1865	

Subject Field	Category	Pattern Heading(s)	
SOCIAL SCIENCES	Industries	Construction industry	H 1153
		Retail trade	
	Types of educational institutions	Universities and colleges	H 1151.5
	Individual educational institutions	Harvard University	H 1151
	Legal topics	Labor laws and legislation	H 1154.5

Subject Field	Category	Pattern Heading(s)	
SCIENCE AND TECHNOLOGY	Land vehicles	Automobiles	H 1195
	Materials	Concrete	H 1158
		Metals	
	Chemicals	Copper	H 1149
		Insulin	
	Organs and regions of the body	Heart	H 1164
		Foot	
	Diseases	Cancer	H 1150
		Tuberculosis	
	Plants and crops	Corn	H 1180
	Animals	Fishes	H 1147
		Cattle	

Subject Field	Category	Pattern Heading(s)	
THE ARTS	Groups of literary authors (including authors, poets, dramatists, etc.)	Authors, English	H 1155.2
	Individual literary authors	Shakespeare, William, 1564-1616	H 1155.4
	Literary works entered under author	Shakespeare, William, 1564-1616. Hamlet	H 1155.6
	Literary works entered under title	Beowulf	H 1155.8
	Languages and groups of languages	English language	H 1154
		French language	
		Romance languages	
	Literatures (including individual genres)	English literature	H 1156
	Newspapers	Newspapers	H 1163
	Music compositions	Operas	H 1160
	Musical instruments	Piano	H 1161

Example: Only One Pattern Heading for the Category

Title	Drought resistance of rice varieties in Thailand

Procedure

1. Rice: But no appropriate subdivision is found.
2. No free-floating subdivision is suitable.
3. Look for the category. Rice belongs to the category Plants and crops. The pattern heading for this category is Corn.
4. Go to Corn in *LCSH* and look for a suitable subdivision. Note all instructions that apply to this heading (e.g., *May Subd Geog*) also apply to the heading you have selected.

Subject heading   **Rice—Thailand—Drought resistance**

EXERCISE 5.1

Using *LCSH*, find appropriate subject headings for the following. Make a note of the pattern heading if used.

Topic	Pattern Heading	Heading
1. The lifecycle of the chipmunk		
2. Longevity of cats		
3. Ellipsis in Albanian		
4. The psychotropic effects of iodine		
5. Economic conditions of Dutch colonies in Asia		
6. Breeding lions		
7. Origins of Zen Buddhism in Japan		
8. Anti-lock brake systems for dune buggies		
9. Diagnosing brain abscesses		

10. Regional variations in the
    macadamia nut industry
    (hint: this is an industry)
    _____   _____

11. Production standards of films
    adapted from Arabic
    children's stories
    _____   _____

12. Research on methods of
    painting of plastics
    _____   _____

13. How French has had an
    impact on English
    _____   _____

14. Genetic engineering of sheep
    in New Zealand
    _____   _____

15. How to deal with vapor lock
    problems in buses
    _____   _____

EXERCISE 5.2

Are the following subject headings correct? If not, indicate a possible correct heading.

Topic	Subject Heading
1. Liver—Size	_____
2. Poets—Exile	_____
3. Spring wheat—Diseases and pests—Italy—Biological Control	_____
4. Sino-French War, 1884-1885—Battles	_____
5. Guitar—Strings—Materials	_____
6. Dogs—Embryos—Canada—Transplantation	_____
7. Llamas—Peru—Handling	_____
8. Toes, Dislocation of	_____

9. Ranunculus—Time of flowering   _____

10. Canola—Disease and pest resistance—Genetic
    aspects   _____

Multiple Subdivisions

A multiple subdivision is a subdivision in *LCSH* that is used to suggest the creation of similar subdivisions under the heading. It is indicated by terms in square brackets generally followed by the word "etc."

The presence of a multiple subdivision under a heading automatically gives free-floating status to similar subdivisions under the same heading, and, if the heading is a pattern heading, under those headings that it controls, e.g.,

World War, 1939-1945—Personal narratives, American, [French, German, etc.]

Possible headings include

World War, 1939-1945—Personal narratives, American
World War, 1939-1945—Personal narratives, French
World War, 1939-1945—Personal narratives, German
World War, 1939-1945—Personal narratives, Australian

The functional equivalent of a multiple subdivision may be presented in the form of a scope note.

Ocean currents
Subdivided by body of water, e.g., Ocean Currents—Atlantic Ocean

Eclipses, Solar
Subdivided by date, e.g., Eclipses, Solar—1854

EXERCISE 5.3

Using *LCSH*, provide a subject heading for each of the following:

Topic	Subject Heading

1. Religious aspects of animal experiments
   from the Islamic viewpoint   _____

2. Subject headings for astronomy   _____

3. Christian beliefs about salt   _____

4. German words and phrases in the English
   language

   _____

5. Buddhist aspects of codependency

   _____

Chapter 6
NAMES

Names

The following types of names can be used as subject headings:

- **personal names**, including names of legendary, mythological and fictitious characters, gods, etc.
- **family names**, including dynasties and royal houses
- **place names** (jurisdictional and nonjurisdictional), including geographic features areas and regions, city sections, early cities, empires, kingdoms, etc.
- **names of corporate bodies**
- **names of art works**
- **names of chemicals, drugs and minerals**
- **biological names**
- other names—e.g., languages (including computer languages), ethnic groups, roads, structures, buildings, railroads, projects, movements, events, trade names, games.

Note: *LCSH* includes personal names, names of corporate bodies, jurisdictional names, and uniform titles only if they require special treatment.

It is always useful to check names in an authority file. Authority files are treated in Chapter 7.

Geographic Names

Geographic names are used in subject cataloging as:

1. Headings
    Australia—Description and travel

2. Subdivisions
    Corn—Iowa

3. Qualifiers
    Yosemite National Park (Calif.)

4. Part of an adjectival or inverted heading
    French drama
    Dramatists, French

Geographic names generally fall into two categories:
- Names for political jurisdictions (e.g., using the name of the geographic area to represent the name of the government)
  i.e., the name as a corporate body, e.g.,
      South Dakota
      Canada

(In this category are included names of countries, provinces, states, cities and towns.)

- Names for areas that are not covered by a political jurisdiction
  i.e., place names, e.g.,
      Everglades National Park (Fla.)
      Chesapeake Bay (Md. and Va.)

In this category are included names of natural geographic features, e.g.,
      Grand Canyon
and built structures, e.g.,
      Golden Gate Bridge.

Jurisdictional Headings
General Rule

Anglo-American cataloguing rules second edition 1988 revision (AACR2R) Chapter 23 gives the basic principles for establishing these names. The *Cataloging service bulletins* of the Library of Congress provide guidance with new names and changes to names.

In brief:
- Use the English form of name if there is one in general use, otherwise the form in the official language of the country (23.2).

- If the name changes, use as many of the names as are required by rules on government names (24.3E). For example, use Cambodia or Kampuchea, as appropriate.

- Check the rules on additions to corporate names (24.4C6) and conference names (24.7B4) or other relevant rules.

- If additions are required to place names, use parentheses.

Identifying between Identical Place Names
- Add a word or phrase commonly used to distinguish them, e.g.,
      Tarbert (Strathclyde, Scotland)
      Tarbert (Western Isles, Scotland)

- If necessary to identify the place (as in the case of a community within a city), give the name of an appropriate smaller place before the name of the specified larger place, e.g.,
  Hyde Park (Chicago, Ill.)
  Chelsea (London, England)

- If the first part of a place name is a term indicating a type of jurisdiction, and the place is commonly listed under another element of its name in lists published in the language of the country in which it is located, omit the term indicating the type of jurisdiction.
  Kerry (Ireland)
  not
  County Kerry (Ireland)

- In all other cases, include the jurisdictional term, e.g.,
  District of Colombia (Mexico City, Mexico)

Non-Jurisdictional Headings

A range of entities can be established as headings. These include:
  Ancient cities
  Archaeological sites, historic sites, etc.
  Areas and regions (when not free-floating)
  Boundary lines
  Bridges
  Canals
  City sections
  Dams
  Farms, ranches, gardens
  Forests, grasslands, etc.
  Geologic basins, geologic formations, etc.
  Mines
  Parks, reserves, refuges, recreation areas, etc.
  Reservoirs
  Roads, streets, trails
  Tunnels

and geographic features including

basins	gorges	plateaus
bays	gulfs	rivers
canyons	lagoons	seas
capes	lakes	sounds
caves	moors	steppes
creeks	mountains	straits
deserts	ocean currents	tonal islands
falls	peninsulas	
fjords	plains	

Geographic Headings That Are Qualified (H 810)

Always qualify by the name of the jurisdiction **except for the following countries:**

Australia	use names of states
Canada	use names of provinces
Great Britain	use names of constituent countries
United States	use names of states
Malaysia	use names of states
Yugoslavia	use names of republics

For a full list of the political divisions for these six exceptions, and the forms to be used as qualifiers, see pp. 8-11 of the *Subject cataloging manual H 810, August 1997 update.*

EXERCISE 6.1

Using *LCSH*, establish the following geographic features as headings.

Topic	**Subject Heading**
1. Hyde Park in Tampa, Florida	_____
2. Isle Royale National Park	_____
3. Royal National Park (south of Sydney)	_____
4. Central Park (in New York)	_____
5. Statue of Liberty	_____
6. Grand Canyon	_____
7. Deerfield Cemetery (in Deerfield, Illinois)	_____
8. Merri River (in Victoria, Australia)	_____
9. London River (in France)	_____
10. Amazon River	_____
11. Death Valley	_____
12. Bond Street (London)	_____
13. 17th Street in Washington	_____
14. Highway 40 (United States)	_____
15. Hilo Bay in Hawaii	_____
16. Brooklyn Bridge (in New York)	_____

17. Westland Park in New Zealand   _____

18. Mount Whitney in California   _____

19. The Sistine Chapel   _____

20. Wailing Wall (in Jerusalem)   _____

EXERCISE 6.2

Using *LCSH*, provide subject headings for the following topics, including geographic subdivisions.

Topic	Subject Heading
1. American libraries	_____
2. Hospitals in Albuquerque	_____
3. A field guide to birds around Billings in Montana	_____
4. Animals in Southeast Asia	_____
5. A report on the police in Kentucky	_____
6. Body surfing on the Gold Coast (Queensland, Australia)	_____
7. Churches in London, Ontario	_____
8. Parakeets of North America	_____
9. Art galleries in Kansas City, Missouri	_____
10. Folk songs of Spain	_____
11. Painters from Rocksprings, Wyoming	_____

12. Research into the climate of Anchorage   _____

13. Bridges in Rome   _____

14. Walking in Richmond, Virginia   _____

15. Education in Vermont   _____

Personal Names
Biography

The biography or autobiography of a person requires the use of a personal name subject heading.

Biography refers to the genre of works consisting of the life histories of individuals, whether written by individuals themselves or by others.

Individual biography refers to a work about the life of one individual. Collective biography refers to a work about the lives of two or more persons.

A complete biography is a work about the life span of one person. A partial biography gives only some details about a person's life.

In order to be considered a biography, a work should present personal details of the biographee, in at least 20% of the available space. Personal details do not include accomplishments, where they lived, who their friends were, etc. Personal details of birth, education, marriage, personal habits and experiences, death and so on should be synthesized and presented as a whole.

Biographical Subdivisions

There are a number of subdivisions that can be used to bring out different aspects of a person's life or work.

- Subdivisions under pattern headings can be used:

  For individual literary authors, use
  > Dante Alighieri, 1265-1321
  > Tolstoy, Leo, Graf 1828-1910
  > Saki, 1870-1916
  > Dwivedi, Mahair Prasad

  For subdivisions to be used under literary works entered under author, use
  > Shakespeare, William, 1564-1616

For subdivisions to be used under literary works entered under title, use
>Beowulf

- Form subdivisions that designate biography
The subdivision —Biography designates individual and collective biography, autobiography, personal reminiscences and personal narratives.

General Rules

- Assign to any biographical work, whether individual or collective, a combination of the following types of headings:
  - [name or names of persons discussed]
  - [class of persons to which the persons discussed belong]—Biography
  - [additional biographical headings for organization, ethnic group, place, event, gender]
  - [additional specific topics, as appropriate]

- Bring out the names of persons discussed (usually only 3 or 4). If a collective biography discusses more than 3 or 4 persons, do not allocate individual name subject headings.

- If a name of head of state or other official, use the personal name, not the corporate head of state heading.

- Use subdivisions from the free-floating subdivisions or pattern headings lists.

- Bring out the subject area or activity that the person is associated with
>[class of person]—[place]—Biography
>e.g.,   Plumbers—Maryland—Biography

- Allocate additional biographical headings where possible to bring out any of the following:
- organization
- ethnic group
- place
- event
- gender.

Partial Biography

If the work treats the life of an individual as one aspect of a fuller treatment, look for personal biographical details of approximately 20%, even if the complete life history is not included. If the personal biography of 20% is not present, still include the name of the person but do not allocate biographical headings. For example,

Title   The personal life of a general during a war

Subject headings   1. Patton, George S. (George Smith), 1885-1945
                         2. World War, 1939-1945—Biography
                         3. Generals—United States—Biography
                         4. United States. Army—Biography

EXERCISE 6.3

Using an authority file, provide a subject heading for each of the following.

Topic	Subject Heading
1. Shakespeare	
2. Antonia Byatt	
3. Bob Hawke	
4. Joan of Arc	
5. Queen Elizabeth II	
6. The Tower of London	
7. The Empire State Building	
8. Agustus Agar	
9. The Tyree Family	
10. Immanuel Kant	

EXERCISE 6.4

Using *LCSH*, provide appropriate subject headings including subdivisions for the following. You may need to check an authority file for the verified forms of names.

Topic	Subject Heading
1. Biography of Earl Warren, a governor of California	
2. Biography of Tony Bennett	
3. A collective biography of the last 10 Presidents of the United States and the events that took place during their tenure	
4. The history of the Pulitzer Prize	
5. The family history of the Taylor family	

Chapter 7
SUBJECT AUTHORITY FILES

Introduction

Authority control is the maintenance of standard forms of headings in the catalog, so that library users can locate information using consistent subject, name and title headings. It also ensures that all future additions to the catalog use the same heading as an access point.

An **authority file** is the record of the correct form of names, series, subjects or uniform titles used in a catalog. It represents a record of decisions made by the cataloger in accordance with the library's policy. It records the standard form of a heading, as prescribed by *AACR2* and all references made to and from the headings.

The largest authority file is *Library of Congress name authorities* which is issued quarterly on microfiche and cumulated annually. It is also issued on CD-ROM, and is available online.

A **subject authority file** is a file of all the subject headings used in the catalog. It also contains references made to the headings. This controls the library's use of subject headings and ensures collocation of records that have the same access point.

An **authority record** is a separate record for each heading. It contains the correct form of the heading, references and notes relating to the reference source used to verify the name.

Two sorts of headings appear in a subject authority file:
* authorized headings/preferred terms that appear in the catalog only
* unauthorized headings/non-preferred terms with a USE reference to the preferred term.

Catalogers normally
1. check for headings used in their catalog
2. if the heading is not found, check an external authority file (e.g., *LCNA*)
3. if not found, check the subject list (e.g., *LCSH*) and construct the required heading
4. perform authority work to include the new heading and any references or links to other headings in the authority file.

A Manual Subject Authority Record

> **Subject Heading**
> Scope note
>
> UF   **Used For:** Non-preferred terms from which Use references will be made to the heading at the top of the card
>
> BT   **Broader Term:** Subject headings from which *see also* references will be made to the heading at the top of the card
>
> RT   **Related Term:** Subject headings to and from which *see also* references will be made to and from the heading at the top of the card
>
> NT   **Narrower Term:** Subject Headings to which a *see also* reference will be made from the subject heading at the top of the card
>
> SA   **See Also:** General *see also* reference
>
>   Reference source

An Online Subject Authority Record

AUTHORITY DISPLAY

COLLECTION ID.ALL

va   voc00-23007 db 07/16/80 12/08/89 ----   ----

Canada Institute for Scientific and Technical Information

      UF   Canada. Institut canadien de l'information scientifique et technique.
      UF   Canada. Institute for Scientific and Technical Information.
      UF   Canadian Institute for Scientific and Technical Information.
      UF   CISTI.
      UF   National Research Council of Canada. Canada Institute for Scientific and Technical Information.

Scope
      In Oct. 16, 1974, the Technical Information Service of the National Research Council of Canada, and the National Science Library merged to form the Canada Institute for Scientific and Technical Information.

Procedures for Creating a Subject Authority Record

The following procedures for establishing a subject authority record and amending the existing subject authority file take you through all types of references. Bear in mind that you may not have to use all the references in the subject headings list. Libraries vary in the extent to which references are made, and the cataloger should always bear in mind the library's cataloging policy.

The procedures are demonstrated using the following example.

Capture at sea
> Here are entered works on enemy property taken at sea. Works
> on the treatment of enemy property taken on land are entered
> under Enemy property
> UF   Captured property
>   Maritime capture
>   Property captured at sea
> BT   Seizure of vessels and cargoes
> RT   Privateering
>   Prize law
> NT   Ransom

1.   Code the subject heading.

        150   0 $aCapture at sea

2.   Include any necessary scope notes.

        150   0 $aCapture at sea
        680           $iHere are entered works on enemy property taken at sea. Works on the treatment of enemy property taken on land are entered under$aEnemy property
        681           $iNote under$aEnemy property

3.   Then add any "seen from" (Used For) references. In this case, there are three.

        150   0 $aCapture at sea
        450   0 $aCaptured property
        450   0 $aMaritime capture
        450   0 $aProperty captured at sea
        680           $iHere are entered works on enemy property taken at sea. Works on the treatment of enemy property taken on land are entered under$aEnemy property
        681           $iNote under$aEnemy property

4.   Then add any "seen also from" references. Note that the code "g" in subfield "w" indicates a Broader Term relationship.

150	0	$aCapture at sea
450	0	$aCaptured property
450	0	$aMaritime capture
450	0	$aProperty captured at sea
550	0	wgaSeizure of vessels and cargoes
680		$iHere are entered works on enemy property taken at sea. Works on the treatment of enemy property taken on land are entered under$aEnemy property
681		$iNote under$aEnemy property

5.   Add related terms if you need them.

150	0	$aCapture at sea
450	0	$aCaptured property
450	0	$aMaritime capture
450	0	$aProperty captured at sea
550	0	wgaSeizure of vessels and cargoes
550	0	$aPrivateering
550	0	$aPrize law

6.   Finally, include a reference(s) to a narrower term(s). Code "h" in subfield "w" indicates the Narrower Term relationship.

150	0	$aCapture at sea
450	0	$aCaptured property
450	0	$aMaritime capture
450	0	$aProperty captured at sea
550	0	wgaSeizure of vessels and cargoes
550	0	$aPrivateering
550	0	$aPrize law
550	0	whaRansom
680		$iHere are entered works on enemy property taken at sea. Works on the treatment of enemy property taken on land are entered under$aEnemy property
681		$iNote under$aEnemy property

The final record is:

150	0	$aCapture at sea
450	0	$aCaptured property
450	0	$aMaritime capture
450	0	$aProperty captured at sea
550	0	wgaSeizure of vessels and cargoes
550	0	$aPrivateering
550	0	$aPrize law
550	0	whaRansom
680		$iHere are entered works on enemy property taken at sea. Works on the treatment of enemy property taken on land are entered under$aEnemy property
681		$iNote under$aEnemy property

7.   Depending on your online system, you may have to go into each of the headings referred to, in order to establish the corresponding reciprocal references.

150	0	$aPrize law
450	0	$aRequisitions (of neutral vessels and cargoes)
450	0	$aShips, Requisition of
550	0	wgaMaritime law
550	0	wgaPrizes
550	0	wgaWar, Maritime (International law)
550	0	$aNeutrality
550	0	$aPrivateering
550	0	$aCapture at sea
150	0	$aPrivateering
450	0	$aCorsairs
550	0	wgaNaval art and science
550	0	wgaNaval history
550	0	wgaPirates
550	0	wgaWar, Maritime (International law)
550	0	$aCapture at sea
550	0	$aLetters of marque
550	0	$aPrize law
150	0	$aSeizure of vessels and cargoes
450	0	$aCargoes, Seizure of
450	0	$aSeizure of cargoes
450	0	$aVessels, Seizure of
550	0	wgaJurisdiction over ships at sea
550	0	wgaMaritime law
550	0	whaCapture at sea

References in the Catalog

In online catalogs, the display of references varies considerably. The corresponding catalog references for the headings above may look like this:

Capture at sea
> Here are entered works on enemy property taken at sea. Works on the treatment of enemy property taken on land are entered under Enemy property

See also Privateering
            Ransom

Captured property

> SEE Capture at Sea

Maritime property

> SEE Capture at Sea

Property captured at sea

> SEE Capture at Sea

Seizure of vessels and cargoes

See also   Angary, Right of
            Contraband of war
            Search, Right of
            Capture at sea

Privateering

See also   Capture at sea
            names of vessels
            Neutrality
            Reprisals

Ransom

See also   Criminal law
            Kidnapping
            Prisoners
            Capture at sea

EXERCISE 7.1

Using *LCSH*, create the necessary Subject Authority record for the heading **Athletics**, and indicate what changes need to be made to existing records.

Athletics *(May Subd Geog)*

UF	College athletics
RT	Physical education and training
	Sports
SA	*subdivision* Athletics *Under names of individual educational institutions,* *e.g.,* Harvard University—Athletics
NT	Boxing
	College sports

Chapter 8
MORE PRACTICE

EXERCISE 8.1

Using *LCSH*, find subject headings, with subdivisions where appropriate, for the following titles.

Topic	Subject Heading
1. AACRII–a computer based training package	
2. Adopted children: a new look at their legal rights	
3. The anti-vivisection movement: a history	
4. The art of growing daffodils	
5. The artists of Spain: works on exhibition	
6. Business English: how to write business letters	
7. Car pools in San Francisco	
8. Carrying out public relations for the Library of Congress	
9. Carrying out library public relations	
10. Maternal and Child Health services in Denmark	
11. Collected biographies of Mexican musicians	
12. Constitutional law in Massachusetts	
13. The cooking of Egypt	
14. Crests and coats of arms: an illustrated guide	
15. A bibliography of education for librarianship	

EXERCISE 8.2

Using *LCSH*, find subject headings, with subdivisions where appropriate, for the following titles.

	Topic	Subject Heading
1.	The effects of pollution on rice-growing	_____
2.	Electricity from the sun	_____
3.	Encyclopedia of the Aztecs	_____
4.	Eroticism in art	_____
5.	Personal stories of American soldiers in the Korean War	_____
6.	Biological treatment of sewage	_____
7.	Grist for the mill: the flour mills of Brazil	_____
8.	Hallelujah I'm a bum: a study of tramps and hobos	_____
9.	Harrap German-Spanish-German dictionary	_____
10.	A history of the People's Republic of China from 1950-1975	_____
11.	House plans by architects	_____
12.	How real is telekinesis?	_____
13.	How to tune a French horn	_____
14.	How to tune a piano	_____
15.	An introduction to Eskimo folksongs	_____

EXERCISE 8.3

Using *LCSH*, find subject headings, with subdivisions where appropriate, for the following titles.

Topic	Subject Heading
1. Medieval history	
2. Telephone directory of Columbus, Nebraska	
3. Mendicants: a history of begging	
4. The model ship catalog	
5. Negotiation in the hostage situation	
6. A new bibliography of fiction about dogs	
7. The dating of porcelain from China	
8. The psychological effects of being unemployed	
9. Relations between Judaism and Islam	
10. Rhymes and poetry for children	
11. Riots and crowd control	
12. The story of the Holy Grail	
13. Snakes of Kentucky	
14. A study of parents without partners	
15. Surfboard riding in Hawaii	

EXERCISE 8.4

Using *LCSH*, find subject headings, with subdivisions where appropriate, for the following titles.

Topic	Subject Heading
1. Surgeons in the Argentine Navy	_____
2. Pilot Creek in Texas	_____
3. An introduction to microcomputers	_____
4. Techniques for photographing insects	_____
5. A collection of photographs of the Vietnam War	_____
6. Television repair manual	_____
7. Public library services to preschoolers	_____
8. Easy dried flower pictures	_____
9. Measuring the earth's gravitational pull	_____
10. The five commandments of Buddhism	_____
11. Judging English riding	_____
12. Transportation of nuclear wastes: legal requirements in Germany	_____
13. Ice-climbing in Nepal	_____
14. When your partner dies	_____
15. Reusing your wastepaper	_____

FREE-FLOATING SUBDIVISIONS (H 1095)

Form and Topical Subdivisions of General Application

—Abbreviations

—Abbreviations of titles

—Ability testing *(May Subd Geog)*

—Abstracting and indexing *(May Subd Geog)*

—Abstracts

—Access control *(May Subd Geog)*

—Accidents *(May Subd Geog)*

—Accidents—Investigation *(May Subd Geog)*

—Accounting

—Accreditation *(May Subd Geog)*

—Acronyms

—Administration

—Aerial photographs

—Air conditioning *(May Subd Geog)*

—Air conditioning—Control *(May Subd Geog)*

—Amateurs' manuals

—Analysis

—Anecdotes

—Anniversaries, etc.

—Archival resources

—Archives

—Art

—Atlases

—Audio-visual aids

—Audio-visual aids—Catalogs

—Audiotape catalogs

—Auditing

—Authorship

—Automatic control

—Automation

—Autonomous communities

—Awards *(May Subd Geog)*

—Biblical teaching

—Bibliography

—Bibliography—Catalogs

—Bibliography—Early

—Bibliography—Exhibitions

—Bibliography—Methodology

—Bibliography—Microform catalogs

—Bibliography—Union lists

—Bio-bibliography

—Biography

—Biography—Dictionaries

—Biography—History and criticism

—Book reviews

—Buildings

—Buildings—Conservation and restoration

—Buildings—Guidebooks

—By-laws

—By-products

—Calendars

—Calibration

—Cantons

—Caricatures and cartoons

—Case studies

—Catalogs

—Catalogs and collections *(May Subd Geog)*

—CD-ROM catalogs

—Censorship *(May Subd Geog)*

—Centennial celebrations, etc.

—Certification *(May Subd Geog)*

—Charitable contributions *(May Subd Geog)*

—Charts, diagrams, etc.

—Chronology

—Citizen participation

—Classification

—Cleaning

—Code numbers

—Code words

—Cold weather conditions

—Collectibles *(May Subd Geog)*

—Collection and preservation

—Collectors and collecting *(May Subd Geog)*

—Colonies

—Comic books, strips, etc.

—Communication systems

—Compact disc catalogs

—Comparative method

—Comparative studies

—Competitions *(May Subd Geog)*

—Composition

—Computer-assisted instruction

—Computer games

—Computer network resources

—Computer networks *(May Subd Geog)*

—Computer networks—Security measures
    (May Subd Geog)

—Computer programs

—Computer simulation

—Concordances

—Congresses

—Congresses—Attendance

—Conservation and restoration

—Control *(May Subd Geog)*

—Controversial literature

—Cooling *(May Subd Geog)*

—Corrosion

—Corrupt practices *(May Subd Geog)*

—Cost control

—Cost effectiveness

—Cost of operation

—Costs

—Cross-cultural studies

—Cult *(May Subd Geog)*

—Curricula

—Customer services *(May Subd Geog)*

—Data processing

—Data tape catalogs

—Databases

—Dating

—Decision making

—Defects *(May Subd Geog)*

—Defects—Reporting *(May Subd Geog)*

—Defense measures *(May Subd Geog)*

—Departments

—Design

—Design and construction

—Design and plans

—Deterioration

—Dictionaries

—Dictionaries—French, [Italian, etc.]

—Dictionaries—Polyglot

—Dictionaries, Juvenile

—Directories

—Discipline

—Discography

—Documentation *(May Subd Geog)*

—Drama

—Drawings

—Drying *(May Subd Geog)*

—Dust control *(May Subd Geog)*

—Early works to 1800

—Econometric models

—Economic aspects *(May Subd Geog)*

—Electromechanical analogies

—Electronic information resources

—Employees

—Encyclopedias

—Encyclopedias, Juvenile

—Endowments

—Energy conservation *(May Subd Geog)*

—Energy consumption *(May Subd Geog)*

—Environmental aspects *(May Subd Geog)*

—Equipment and supplies

—Estimates *(May Subd Geog)*

—Evaluation

—Examinations

—Examinations—Study guides

—Examinations, questions, etc.

—Exhibitions

—Experiments

—Facsimiles

—Fiction

—Field work

—Film catalogs

—Finance

—Fires and fire prevention *(May Subd Geog)*

—Folklore

—Food service *(May Subd Geog)*

—Forecasting

—Foreign countries

—Foreign influences

—Forgeries *(May Subd Geog)*

—Forms

—Fume control *(May Subd Geog)*

—Government policy *(May Subd Geog)*

—Grading *(May Subd Geog)*

—Graphic methods

—Guidebooks

—Handbooks, manuals, etc.

—Health aspects *(May Subd Geog)*

—Heating and ventilation *(May Subd Geog)*

—Heating and ventilation—Control
  (May Subd Geog)

—Heraldry

—Historiography

—History

—History—16th century

—History—17th century

—History—18th century

—History—19th century

—History—20th century

—History—Chronology

—History—Philosophy

—History—Sources

—History and criticism

—History of doctrines

—History of doctrines—Early church, ca. 30-600

—History of doctrines—Middle Ages, 600-1500

—History of doctrines—16th century

—History of doctrines—17th century

—History of doctrines—18th century

—History of doctrines—19th century

—History of doctrines—20th century

—Hot weather conditions *(May Subd Geog)*

—Humor

—Identification

—Illustrations

—Indexes

—Industrial applications *(May Subd Geog)*

—Influence

—Information resources

—Information services

—Insignia

—Inspection *(May Subd Geog)*

—Instruments

—Interactive multimedia

—International cooperation

—Interpretation

—Inventories

—Inventory control *(May Subd Geog)*

—Job descriptions *(May Subd Geog)*

—Juvenile drama

—Juvenile fiction

—Juvenile films

—Juvenile humor

—Juvenile literature

—Juvenile poetry

—Juvenile software

—Juvenile sound recordings

—Labeling *(May Subd Geog)*

—Labor productivity *(May Subd Geog)*

—Laboratory manuals

—Language

—Legends

—Library resources

—Licenses *(May Subd Geog)*

—Licenses—Fees *(May Subd Geog)*

—Lighting *(May Subd Geog)*

—Linear programming

—Literary collections

—Location *(May Subd Geog)*

—Longitudinal studies

—Maintenance and repair

—Management

—Manuscripts

—Manuscripts—Catalogs

—Manuscripts—Facsimiles

—Manuscripts—Indexes

—Manuscripts—Microform catalogs

—Maps

—Maps—Bibliography

—Maps—Early works to 1800

—Maps—Facsimiles

—Maps—Symbols

—Maps, Comparative

—Maps, Manuscript

—Maps, Mental

—Maps, Outline and base

—Maps, Physical

—Maps, Pictorial

—Maps, Topographic

—Maps, Tourist

—Maps for children

—Maps for the blind

—Maps for the visually handicapped

—Marketing

—Materials

—Mathematical models

—Mathematics

—Measurement

—Medals *(May Subd Geog)*

—Medical examinations *(May Subd Geog)*

—Meditations

—Membership

—Methodology

—Microform catalogs

—Miscellaneous

—Models *(May Subd Geog)*

—Moisture *(May Subd Geog)*

—Moral and ethical aspects *(May Subd Geog)*

—Museums *(May Subd Geog)*

—Name

—Names

—Newspapers

—Noise

—Nomenclature

—Nomograms

—Notation

—Observations

—Observers' manuals

—Officials and employees

—On postage stamps

—Outlines, syllabi, etc.

—Packaging

—Packing *(May Subd Geog)*

—Papal documents

—Parodies, imitations, etc.

—Patents

—Periodicals

—Periodicals—Abbreviations of titles

—Periodicals—Bibliography

—Periodicals—Bibliography—Catalogs

—Periodicals—Bibliography—Union lists

—Periodicals—Indexes

—Personal narratives

—Personnel management

—Philosophy

—Photographs

—Photographs from space

—Physiological aspects

—Physiological effect

—Pictorial works

—Planning

—Poetry

—Political activity

—Political aspects *(May Subd Geog)*

—Popular works

—Posters

—Power supply *(May Subd Geog)*

—Practice *(May Subd Geog)*

—Prayer-books and devotions

—Prayer-books and devotions—History and criticism

—Preservation *(May Subd Geog)*

—Press coverage *(May Subd Geog)*

—Prevention

—Prices *(May Subd Geog)*

—Prices—Government policy *(May Subd Geog)*

—Private collections *(May Subd Geog)*

—Privileges and immunities

—Problems, exercises, etc.

—Production control *(May Subd Geog)*

—Production standards *(May Subd Geog)*

—Programmed instruction

—Programming

—Prophecies

—Protection *(May Subd Geog)*

—Provinces

—Psychological aspects

—Psychology

—Public opinion

—Publishing *(May Subd Geog)*

—Purchasing *(May Subd Geog)*

—Quality control

—Quotations, maxims, etc.

—Rates *(May Subd Geog)*

—Records and correspondence

—Recreational use

—Regional disparities

—Regions

—Registers

—Reliability

—Religion

—Remodeling *(May Subd Geog)*

—Remote sensing

—Remote-sensing maps

—Repairing *(May Subd Geog)*

—Republics

—Research *(May Subd Geog)*

—Research grants *(May Subd Geog)*

—Reviews

—Romances

—Rules

—Rules and practice

—Safety appliances *(May Subd Geog)*

—Safety measures

—Safety regulations *(May Subd Geog)*

—Sanitation

—Scholarships, fellowships, etc. *(May Subd Geog)*

—Scientific applications *(May Subd Geog)*

—Security measures *(May Subd Geog)*

—Sermons

—Sex differences

—Simulation methods

—Slang

—Slides

—Social aspects *(May Subd Geog)*

—Societies, etc.

—Sociological aspects

—Software

—Songs and music

—Sources

—Specifications *(May Subd Geog)*

—Specimens

—Spectra

—Speeches in Congress

—Stability

—Standards *(May Subd Geog)*

—State supervision

—States

—Statistical methods

—Statistical services

—Statistics

—Storage *(May Subd Geog)*

—Study and teaching *(May Subd Geog)*

—Study and teaching—Activity programs *(May Subd Geog)*

—Study and teaching—Audio-visual aids

—Study and teaching—Simulation methods

—Study and teaching—Supervision *(May Subd Geog)*

—Study and teaching (Continuing education) *(May Subd Geog)*

—Study and teaching (Continuing education)—Audio-visual aids

—Study and teaching (Early childhood) *(May Subd Geog)*

—Study and teaching (Early childhood)—Activity programs

—Study and teaching (Early childhood)—Audio-visual aids

—Study and teaching (Elementary) *(May Subd Geog)*

—Study and teaching (Elementary)—Activity programs *(May Subd Geog)*

—Study and teaching (Elementary)—Audio-visual aids

—Study and teaching (Elementary)—Simulation methods

—Study and teaching (Graduate) *(May Subd Geog)*

—Study and teaching (Higher) *(May Subd Geog)*

—Study and teaching (Higher)—Activity programs *(May Subd Geog)*

—Study and teaching (Higher)—Audio-visual aids

—Study and teaching (Higher)—Simulation methods

—Study and teaching (Internship) *(May Subd Geog)*

—Study and teaching (Middle school) *(May Subd Geog)*

—Study and teaching (Middle school)—Audio-visual aids

—Study and teaching (Preschool) *(May Subd Geog)*

—Study and teaching (Preschool)—Activity programs *(May Subd Geog)*

—Study and teaching (Preschool)—Audio-visual aids

—Study and teaching (Primary) *(May Subd Geog)*

—Study and teaching (Primary)—Activity programs *(May Subd Geog)*

—Study and teaching (Primary)—Audio-visual aids

—Study and teaching (Residency) *(May Subd Geog)*

—Study and teaching (Secondary) *(May Subd Geog)*

—Study and teaching (Secondary)—Activity programs *(May Subd Geog)*

—Study and teaching (Secondary)—Audio-visual aids

—Study and teaching (Secondary)—Simulation methods

—Study guides

—Tables

—Taxation *(May Subd Geog)*

—Technique

—Technological innovations *(May Subd Geog)*

—Telephone directories

—Terminology

—Terminology—Pronunciation

—Territories and possessions

—Testing

—Textbooks

—Texts

—Themes, motives

—Therapeutic use *(May Subd Geog)*

—Tombs

—Toxicology *(May Subd Geog)*

—Trademarks

—Translating

—Translations

—Translations into [name of language]

—Translations into [name of language]—Bibliography

—Transportation *(May Subd Geog)*

—Tropical conditions

—Union lists

—Union territories

—Validity *(May Subd Geog)*

—Valuation *(May Subd Geog)*

—Vibration *(May Subd Geog)*

—Video catalogs

—Vocational guidance *(May Subd Geog)*

—Waste disposal *(May Subd Geog)*

—Waste minimization *(May Subd Geog)*

—Water-supply

—Weight

—Weights and measures

PATTERN HEADINGS

Organs and Regions of the Body (H 1164)

Patterns: Foot; Heart

—Abnormalities *(May Subd Geog)*

—Abscess *(May Subd Geog)*

—Acupuncture *(May Subd Geog)*

—Aging

—Aging—Molecular aspects

—Anatomy

—Ankylosis *(May Subd Geog)*

—Biopsy *(May Subd Geog)*

—Blood-vessels

—Blunt trauma *(May Subd Geog)*

—Calcification *(May Subd Geog)*

—Cancer *(May Subd Geog)*

—Care and hygiene *(May Subd Geog)*

—Contraction *(May Subd Geog)*

—Cryopreservation *(May Subd Geog)*

—Cryosurgery *(May Subd Geog)*

—Cultures and culture media *(May Subd Geog)*

—Cysts *(May Subd Geog)*

—Cytochemistry

—Cytology

—Cytopathology

—Differentiation

—Dilatation *(May Subd Geog)*

—Diseases *(May Subd Geog)*

—Dislocation *(May Subd Geog)*

—Displacement

—Dissection *(May Subd Geog)*

—Effect of chemicals on *(May Subd Geog)*

—Effect of cold on *(May Subd Geog)*

—Effect of drugs on *(May Subd Geog)*

—Effect of heat on *(May Subd Geog)*

—Effect of implants on *(May Subd Geog)*

—Effect of metals on *(May Subd Geog)*

—Effect of radiation on *(May Subd Geog)*

—Effect of space flight on

—Effect of vibration on *(May Subd Geog)*

—Electric properties *(May Subd Geog)*

—Endoscopic surgery *(May Subd Geog)*

—Endoscopic surgery—Complications
  (May Subd Geog)

—Evolution *(May Subd Geog)*

—Examination

—Fibrosis *(May Subd Geog)*

—Foreign bodies *(May Subd Geog)*

—Fractures *(May Subd Geog)*

—Growth

—Growth—Molecular aspects

—Growth—Regulation

—Hemorrhage *(May Subd Geog)*

—Histochemistry

—Histology

—Histopathology

—Hydatids

—Hypertrophy *(May Subd Geog)*

—Imaging *(May Subd Geog)*

—Immunology

—Infections *(May Subd Geog)*

—Innervation

—Interventional radiology *(May Subd Geog)*

—Laser surgery *(May Subd Geog)*

—Laser surgery—Instruments

—Lymphatics

—Magnetic fields

—Magnetic resonance imaging *(May Subd Geog)*

—Massage *(May Subd Geog)*

—Mechanical properties

—Metabolism

—Metabolism—Disorders *(May Subd Geog)*

—Metabolism—Endocrine aspects

—Metabolism—Regulation

—Microbiology *(May Subd Geog)*

—Microscopy *(May Subd Geog)*

—Models *(May Subd Geog)*

—Molecular aspects

—Movements

—Muscles

—Mythology *(May Subd Geog)*

—Necrosis *(May Subd Geog)*

—Needle biopsy *(May Subd Geog)*

—Paralysis

—Parasites *(May Subd Geog)*

—Pathophysiology

—Permeability

—Phylogeny

—Physiology

—Precancerous conditions *(May Subd Geog)*

—Preservation *(May Subd Geog)*

—Protection *(May Subd Geog)*

—Psychophysiology

—Radiation injuries *(May Subd Geog)*

—Radiography *(May Subd Geog)*

—Radiography—Law and legislation
  (May Subd Geog)

—Radiography—Positioning *(May Subd Geog)*

—Radionuclide imaging *(May Subd Geog)*

—Regeneration *(May Subd Geog)*

—Reimplantation

—Religious aspects

—Religious aspects—Buddhism, [Christianity, etc.]

—Reoperation *(May Subd Geog)*

—Rupture *(May Subd Geog)*

—Secretions

—Sex differences

—Size *(May Subd Geog)*

—Sounds

—Spectroscopic imaging *(May Subd Geog)*

—Surgery *(May Subd Geog)*

—Surgery—Complications *(May Subd Geog)*

—Surgery—Instruments

—Surgery—Instruments—Sterilization

—Surgery—Nursing *(May Subd Geog)*

—Surgery—Nutritional aspects

—Surgery—Patients *(May Subd Geog)*

—Surgery—Risk factors *(May Subd Geog)*

—Symbolic aspects *(May Subd Geog)*

—Syphilis *(May Subd Geog)*

—Thermography

—Tomography

—Traction *(May Subd Geog)*

—Transplantation *(May Subd Geog)*

—Transplantation—Complications
  (May Subd Geog)

—Transplantation—Immunological aspects

—Transplantation—Law and legislation
(May Subd Geog)

—Transplantation—Nursing *(May Subd Geog)*

—Transplantation—Patients *(May Subd Geog)*

—Tuberculosis *(May Subd Geog)*

—Tumors *(May Subd Geog)*

—Ulcers *(May Subd Geog)*

—Ultrasonic imaging *(May Subd Geog)*

—Ultrastructure

—Weight

—Wounds and injuries *(May Subd Geog)*

Plants and Crops (H 1180)

Pattern: Corn

—Abnormalities *(May Subd Geog)*

—Adaptation *(May Subd Geog)*

—Age

—Aging

—Aging—Genetic aspects

—Analysis

—Anatomy

—Biological control *(May Subd Geog)*

—Biotechnology *(May Subd Geog)*

—Breeding *(May Subd Geog)*

—Catalogs and collections *(May Subd Geog)*

—Chemotaxonomy

—Cladistic analysis *(May Subd Geog)*

—Classification

—Climatic factors *(May Subd Geog)*

—Clones *(May Subd Geog)*

—Clones—Selection *(May Subd Geog)*

—Clones—Variation *(May Subd Geog)*

—Color *(May Subd Geog)*

—Color—Fading *(May Subd Geog)*

—Color—Fading—Control *(May Subd Geog)*

—Color—Genetic aspects

—Composition

—Control *(May Subd Geog)*

—Control—Environmental aspects
   (May Subd Geog)

—Control—Law and legislation *(May Subd Geog)*

—Cooling *(May Subd Geog)*

—Cooperative marketing *(May Subd Geog)*

—Cultural control *(May Subd Geog)*

—Cuttings *(May Subd Geog)*

—Cytochemistry

—Cytogenetics

—Cytology

—Cytotaxonomy

—Development

—Disease and pest resistance *(May Subd Geog)*

—Disease and pest resistance—Genetic aspects

—Disease-free stock *(May Subd Geog)*

—Diseases and pests *(May Subd Geog)*

—Diseases and pests—Biological control
   (May Subd Geog)

—Diseases and pests—Control *(May Subd Geog)*

—Diseases and pests—Control—Environmental
   aspects *(May Subd Geog)*

—Diseases and pests—Cultural control
   (May Subd Geog)

—Diseases and pests—Identification
   (May Subd Geog)

—Diseases and pests—Integrated control
   (May Subd Geog)

—Diseases and pests—Monitoring
   (May Subd Geog)

—Dispersal *(May Subd Geog)*

—Dormancy *(May Subd Geog)*

—Drought tolerance *(May Subd Geog)*

—Drying *(May Subd Geog)*

—Ecology *(May Subd Geog)*

—Ecophysiology *(May Subd Geog)*

—Effect of acid deposition on *(May Subd Geog)*

—Effect of acid precipitation on *(May Subd Geog)*

—Effect of air pollution on *(May Subd Geog)*

—Effect of air pollution on—Genetic aspects

—Effect of arsenic on *(May Subd Geog)*

—Effect of atmospheric carbon dioxide on
   (May Subd Geog)

—Effect of atmospheric deposition on
     (May Subd Geog)

—Effect of atmospheric nitrogen dioxide on
     (May Subd Geog)

—Effect of atmospheric ozone on *(May Subd Geog)*

—Effect of cadmium on *(May Subd Geog)*

—Effect of cold on *(May Subd Geog)*

—Effect of drought on *(May Subd Geog)*

—Effect of ethephon on *(May Subd Geog)*

—Effect of factory and trade waste on
     (May Subd Geog)

—Effect of ferrous sulfate on *(May Subd Geog)*

—Effect of fires on *(May Subd Geog)*

—Effect of floods on *(May Subd Geog)*

—Effect of fluorine on *(May Subd Geog)*

—Effect of freezes on *(May Subd Geog)*

—Effect of gamma rays on *(May Subd Geog)*

—Effect of global warming on *(May Subd Geog)*

—Effect of glyphosate on *(May Subd Geog)*

—Effect of heavy metals on *(May Subd Geog)*

—Effect of magnesium on *(May Subd Geog)*

—Effect of minerals on *(May Subd Geog)*

—Effect of oxygen on *(May Subd Geog)*

—Effect of ozone on *(May Subd Geog)*

—Effect of pollution on *(May Subd Geog)*

—Effect of radiation on *(May Subd Geog)*

—Effect of radioactive pollution on
     (May Subd Geog)

—Effect of salt on *(May Subd Geog)*

—Effect of soil acidity on *(May Subd Geog)*

—Effect of stress on *(May Subd Geog)*

—Effect of temperature on *(May Subd Geog)*

—Effect of thermal pollution on *(May Subd Geog)*

—Effect of trampling on *(May Subd Geog)*

—Effect of turbidity on *(May Subd Geog)*

—Effect of volcanic eruptions on *(May Subd Geog)*

—Effect of water pollution on *(May Subd Geog)*

—Effect of wind on *(May Subd Geog)*

—Electric properties *(May Subd Geog)*

—Embryology

—Embryos

—Embryos—Nutrition

—Equipment and supplies

—Evolution *(May Subd Geog)*

—Fertilizers *(May Subd Geog)*

—Field experiments

—Flowering

—Flowering time

—Frost damage *(May Subd Geog)*

—Frost protection *(May Subd Geog)*

—Frost resistance *(May Subd Geog)*

—Fumigation *(May Subd Geog)*

—Genetic engineering *(May Subd Geog)*

—Genetics

—Geographical distribution

—Germplasm resources *(May Subd Geog)*

—Germplasm resources—Catalogs and collections
     (May Subd Geog)

—Germplasm resources—Cryopreservation
     (May Subd Geog)

—Gift books

—Grading *(May Subd Geog)*

—Grafting *(May Subd Geog)*

—Growth

—Habitat *(May Subd Geog)*

—Handling *(May Subd Geog)*

—Hardiness *(May Subd Geog)*

—Harvesting *(May Subd Geog)*

—Harvesting—Machinery *(May Subd Geog)*

—Harvesting time *(May Subd Geog)*

—Health *(May Subd Geog)*

—Heirloom varieties *(May Subd Geog)*

—Herbicide injuries *(May Subd Geog)*

—Histochemistry

—Husking *(May Subd Geog)*

—Identification

—Industrial applications *(May Subd Geog)*

—Inoculation *(May Subd Geog)*

—Insect resistance *(May Subd Geog)*

—Inspection *(May Subd Geog)*

—Integrated control *(May Subd Geog)*

—Irrigation *(May Subd Geog)*

—Judging *(May Subd Geog)*

—Law and legislation *(May Subd Geog)*

—Life cycles *(May Subd Geog)*

—Location *(May Subd Geog)*

—Longevity *(May Subd Geog)*

—Losses *(May Subd Geog)*

—Losses—Prevention

—Machinery *(May Subd Geog)*

—Marketing

—Mechanical properties

—Metabolism

—Microbiology *(May Subd Geog)*

—Micropropagation *(May Subd Geog)*

—Microscopy *(May Subd Geog)*

—Milling *(May Subd Geog)*

—Moisture *(May Subd Geog)*

—Molecular aspects

—Molecular genetics

—Monitoring *(May Subd Geog)*

—Morphogenesis *(May Subd Geog)*

—Morphology

—Mutation breeding *(May Subd Geog)*

—Mythology *(May Subd Geog)*

—Nomenclature

—Nomenclature (Popular)

—Nutrition

—Origin

—Osmotic potential *(May Subd Geog)*

—Packaging

—Packing *(May Subd Geog)*

—Phenology

—Photomorphogenesis

—Phylogeny

—Physiological effect

—Physiology

—Planting *(May Subd Geog)*

—Planting time *(May Subd Geog)*

—Pollen *(May Subd Geog)*

—Pollen—Morphology

—Pollen management *(May Subd Geog)*

—Postharvest diseases and injuries *(May Subd Geog)*

—Postharvest diseases and injuries—Biological control *(May Subd Geog)*

—Postharvest diseases and injuries—Integrated control *(May Subd Geog)*

—Postharvest losses *(May Subd Geog)*

—Postharvest losses—Prevention

—Postharvest physiology *(May Subd Geog)*

—Postharvest technology *(May Subd Geog)*

—Precooling *(May Subd Geog)*

—Preharvest sprouting *(May Subd Geog)*

—Preservation *(May Subd Geog)*

—Prices *(May Subd Geog)*

—Processing *(May Subd Geog)*

—Processing—Machinery *(May Subd Geog)*

—Propagation *(May Subd Geog)*

—Protection *(May Subd Geog)*

—Provenance trials *(May Subd Geog)*

—Provenances *(May Subd Geog)*

—Pruning *(May Subd Geog)*

—Psychic aspects *(May Subd Geog)*

—Quality

—Radiation preservation

—Radioactive contamination *(May Subd Geog)*

—Radiography *(May Subd Geog)*

—Religious aspects

—Religious aspects—Baptists,
   [Catholic Church, etc.]

—Religious aspects—Buddhism, [Christianity, etc.]

—Reproduction

—Research *(May Subd Geog)*

—Research—Law and legislation *(May Subd Geog)*

—Residues *(May Subd Geog)*

—Ripening *(May Subd Geog)*

—Roots

—Roots—Anatomy

—Roots—Physiology

—Rootstocks *(May Subd Geog)*

—Sampling *(May Subd Geog)*

—Seasonal variations *(May Subd Geog)*

—Seedlings

—Seedlings—Ecophysiology *(May Subd Geog)*

—Seedlings—Evaluation *(May Subd Geog)*

—Seedlings—Protection *(May Subd Geog)*

—Seedlings—Quality

—Seedlings—Roots

—Seedlings, Bareroot

—Seedlings, Container

—Seeds

—Seeds—Dormancy *(May Subd Geog)*

—Seeds—Handling *(May Subd Geog)*

—Seeds—Harvesting *(May Subd Geog)*

—Seeds—Identification

—Seeds—Marketing

—Seeds—Morphology

—Seeds—Packaging

—Seeds—Physiology

—Seeds—Postharvest technology *(May Subd Geog)*

—Seeds—Processing *(May Subd Geog)*

—Seeds—Quality

—Seeds—Storage *(May Subd Geog)*

—Seeds—Testing

—Seeds—Viability *(May Subd Geog)*

—Selection *(May Subd Geog)*

—Sensory evaluation *(May Subd Geog)*

—Shelling *(May Subd Geog)*

—Shelling—Machinery *(May Subd Geog)*

—Showing *(May Subd Geog)*

—Silage *(May Subd Geog)*

—Soils *(May Subd Geog)*

—Somatic embryogenesis *(May Subd Geog)*

—Sowing *(May Subd Geog)*

—Spacing *(May Subd Geog)*

—Speciation *(May Subd Geog)*

—Storage *(May Subd Geog)*

—Storage—Climatic factors *(May Subd Geog)*

—Storage—Diseases and injuries *(May Subd Geog)*

—Technological innovations *(May Subd Geog)*

—Temperature

—Therapeutic use *(May Subd Geog)*

—Therapeutic use—Side effects *(May Subd Geog)*

—Thermal properties *(May Subd Geog)*

—Thermal properties—Measurement

—Thinning *(May Subd Geog)*

—Toxicology *(May Subd Geog)*

—Training *(May Subd Geog)*

—Transplanting *(May Subd Geog)*

—Transplanting—Machinery *(May Subd Geog)*

—Transportation *(May Subd Geog)*

—Transportation—Diseases and injuries
    (May Subd Geog)

—Type specimens *(May Subd Geog)*

—Ultrastructure

—Utilization *(May Subd Geog)*

—Varieties *(May Subd Geog)*

—Vegetative propagation *(May Subd Geog)*

—Vitality *(May Subd Geog)*

—Water requirements *(May Subd Geog)*

—Weed control *(May Subd Geog)*

—Wounds and injuries *(May Subd Geog)*

—Wounds and injuries—Diagnosis
    (May Subd Geog)

—Yields *(May Subd Geog)*

Animals (H 1147)

Pattern: Fishes; Cattle

—Abnormalities *(May Subd Geog)*

—Adaptation *(May Subd Geog)*

—Age

—Age determination

—Aging

—Anatomy

—Artificial insemination *(May Subd Geog)*

—Artificial spawning *(May Subd Geog)*

—Autopsy *(May Subd Geog)*

—Behavior *(May Subd Geog)*

—Behavior—Climatic factors *(May Subd Geog)*

—Behavior—Evolution *(May Subd Geog)*

—Biography

—Biological control *(May Subd Geog)*

—Breeding *(May Subd Geog)*

—Breeding—Selection indexes

—Buying

—Carcasses *(May Subd Geog)*

—Carcasses—Grading *(May Subd Geog)*

—Cardiovascular system

—Catalogs and collections *(May Subd Geog)*

—Classification

—Climatic factors *(May Subd Geog)*

—Collection and preservation

—Color *(May Subd Geog)*

—Composition

—Condition scoring *(May Subd Geog)*

—Conformation *(May Subd Geog)*

—Control *(May Subd Geog)*

—Control—Environmental aspects
  (May Subd Geog)

—Control—Law and legislation *(May Subd Geog)*

—Cooperative marketing *(May Subd Geog)*

—Counting *(May Subd Geog)*

—Cultural control *(May Subd Geog)*

—Cytogenetics

—Cytology

—Development

—Digestive organs

—Diseases *(May Subd Geog)*

—Diseases—Alternative treatment *(May Subd Geog)*

—Diseases—Chemotherapy *(May Subd Geog)*

—Diseases—Chiropractic treatment
  (May Subd Geog)

—Diseases—Diagnosis *(May Subd Geog)*

—Diseases—Diet therapy *(May Subd Geog)*

—Diseases—Epidemiology *(May Subd Geog)*

—Diseases—Genetic aspects

—Diseases—Nursing *(May Subd Geog)*

—Diseases—Nutritional aspects

—Diseases—Prevention

—Diseases—Treatment *(May Subd Geog)*

—Dispersal *(May Subd Geog)*

—Dissection *(May Subd Geog)*

—Ecology *(May Subd Geog)*

—Ecophysiology *(May Subd Geog)*

—Effect of chemicals on *(May Subd Geog)*

—Effect of cold on *(May Subd Geog)*

—Effect of dams on *(May Subd Geog)*

—Effect of drought on *(May Subd Geog)*

—Effect of fires on *(May Subd Geog)*

—Effect of habitat modification on
  (May Subd Geog)

—Effect of heavy metals on *(May Subd Geog)*

—Effect of insecticides on *(May Subd Geog)*

—Effect of light on *(May Subd Geog)*

—Effect of logging on *(May Subd Geog)*

—Effect of metals on *(May Subd Geog)*

—Effect of noise on *(May Subd Geog)*

—Effect of oil spills on *(May Subd Geog)*

—Effect of pesticides on *(May Subd Geog)*

—Effect of pollution on *(May Subd Geog)*

—Effect of radiation on *(May Subd Geog)*

—Effect of salt on *(May Subd Geog)*

—Effect of sediments on *(May Subd Geog)*

—Effect of storms on

—Effect of stray currents on *(May Subd Geog)*

—Effect of stress on *(May Subd Geog)*

—Effect of temperature on *(May Subd Geog)*

—Effect of turbidity on *(May Subd Geog)*

—Effect of volcanic eruptions on *(May Subd Geog)*

—Effect of water levels on *(May Subd Geog)*

—Effect of water pollution on *(May Subd Geog)*

—Effect of water quality on *(May Subd Geog)*

—Eggs *(May Subd Geog)*

—Eggs—Counting *(May Subd Geog)*

—Eggs—Incubation *(May Subd Geog)*

—Embryos

—Embryos—Anatomy

—Embryos—Physiology

—Embryos—Transplantation *(May Subd Geog)*

—Environmental enrichment *(May Subd Geog)*

—Equipment and supplies

—Evolution *(May Subd Geog)*

—Exercise *(May Subd Geog)*

—Exercise—Physiological aspects

—Feed utilization efficiency *(May Subd Geog)*

—Feeding and feeds *(May Subd Geog)*

—Feeding and feeds—Climatic factors *(May Subd Geog)*

—Feeding and feeds—Contamination *(May Subd Geog)*

—Feeding and feeds—Equipment and supplies

—Fertility *(May Subd Geog)*

—Fetuses

—Fetuses—Anatomy

—Fetuses—Physiology

—Food *(May Subd Geog)*

—Fractures *(May Subd Geog)*

—Generative organs

—Genetic engineering *(May Subd Geog)*

—Genetics

—Genome mapping *(May Subd Geog)*

—Geographical distribution

—Germplasm resources *(May Subd Geog)*

—Germplasm resources—Cryopreservation *(May Subd Geog)*

—Germplasm resources—Microbiology *(May Subd Geog)*

—Grading *(May Subd Geog)*

—Grooming *(May Subd Geog)*

—Growth

—Habitat *(May Subd Geog)*

—Habitations *(May Subd Geog)*

—Handling *(May Subd Geog)*

—Health *(May Subd Geog)*

—Hibernation *(May Subd Geog)*

—Histology

—Histopathology

—Homing *(May Subd Geog)*

—Host plants *(May Subd Geog)*

—Housing *(May Subd Geog)*

—Housing—Air conditioning *(May Subd Geog)*

—Housing—Decoration *(May Subd Geog)*

—Housing—Design and construction

—Housing—Disinfection *(May Subd Geog)*

—Housing—Environmental engineering
  (May Subd Geog)

—Housing—Insulation *(May Subd Geog)*

—Housing—Lighting *(May Subd Geog)*

—Housing—Odor control *(May Subd Geog)*

—Housing—Safety measures

—Housing—Sanitation *(May Subd Geog)*

—Housing—Specifications *(May Subd Geog)*

—Housing—Waste disposal *(May Subd Geog)*

—Identification

—Immunology

—Immunology—Genetic aspects

—Induced spawning

—Infancy *(May Subd Geog)*

—Infections *(May Subd Geog)*

—Infertility *(May Subd Geog)*

—Inspection *(May Subd Geog)*

—Inspection—Risk assessment *(May Subd Geog)*

—Integrated control *(May Subd Geog)*

—Judging *(May Subd Geog)*

—Larvae *(May Subd Geog)*

—Larvae—Disposal *(May Subd Geog)*

—Larvae—Ecology *(May Subd Geog)*

—Law and legislation *(May Subd Geog)*

—Life cycles *(May Subd Geog)*

—Locomotion *(May Subd Geog)*

—Longevity *(May Subd Geog)*

—Losses *(May Subd Geog)*

—Manure *(May Subd Geog)*

—Manure—Environmental aspects
  (May Subd Geog)

—Manure—Handling *(May Subd Geog)*

—Metabolism

—Metabolism—Climatic factors *(May Subd Geog)*

—Microbiology *(May Subd Geog)*

—Migration *(May Subd Geog)*

—Migration—Climatic factors *(May Subd Geog)*

—Molecular aspects

—Molecular genetics

—Monitoring *(May Subd Geog)*

—Morphogenesis *(May Subd Geog)*

—Morphology

—Mortality

—Mythology *(May Subd Geog)*

—Names

—Nervous system

—Nests *(May Subd Geog)*

—Nomenclature

—Nomenclature (Popular)

—Nutrition

—Nutrition—Requirements

—Odor *(May Subd Geog)*

—Orientation *(May Subd Geog)*

—Origin

—Parasites *(May Subd Geog)*

—Parasites—Biological control *(May Subd Geog)*

—Parasites—Control—Environmental aspects
  (May Subd Geog)

—Parasites—Identification

—Parasites—Life cycles *(May Subd Geog)*

—Parturition *(May Subd Geog)*

—Pathogens *(May Subd Geog)*

—Pedigrees

—Performance records

—Phylogeny

—Physiology

—Pregnancy *(May Subd Geog)*

—Productivity *(May Subd Geog)*

—Psychic aspects

—Psychological testing *(May Subd Geog)*

—Psychology

—Quality

—Racial analysis *(May Subd Geog)*

—Religious aspects

—Religious aspects—Buddhism, [Christianity, etc.]

—Reproduction

—Reproduction—Climatic factors *(May Subd Geog)*

—Reproduction—Endocrine aspects

—Reproduction—Regulation

—Respiration

—Respiratory organs

—Schooling

—Seasonal distribution *(May Subd Geog)*

—Selection *(May Subd Geog)*

—Sense organs

—Services for *(May Subd Geog)*

—Sexing *(May Subd Geog)*

—Showing *(May Subd Geog)*

—Size *(May Subd Geog)*

—Spawning *(May Subd Geog)*

—Speciation *(May Subd Geog)*

—Speed

—Spermatozoa

—Spermatozoa—Abnormalities *(May Subd Geog)*

—Spermatozoa—Morphology

—Stranding *(May Subd Geog)*

—Summering *(May Subd Geog)*

—Surgery *(May Subd Geog)*

—Surgery—Complications *(May Subd Geog)*

—Surgery—Nursing *(May Subd Geog)*

—Symbolic aspects *(May Subd Geog)*

—Technological innovations *(May Subd Geog)*

—Testing

—Therapeutic use *(May Subd Geog)*

—Toxicology *(May Subd Geog)*

—Training *(May Subd Geog)*

—Transportation *(May Subd Geog)*

—Trypanotolerance

—Type specimens *(May Subd Geog)*

—Vaccination *(May Subd Geog)*

—Variation *(May Subd Geog)*

—Venom *(May Subd Geog)*

—Vertical distribution *(May Subd Geog)*

—Virus diseases *(May Subd Geog)*

—Viruses *(May Subd Geog)*

—Vocalization *(May Subd Geog)*

—Vocalization—Regulation

—Water requirements *(May Subd Geog)*

—Weight

—Wintering *(May Subd Geog)*

—Wounds and injuries *(May Subd Geog)*

ANSWERS

Note: These answers have been verified in the 20th edition of *LCSH* and the 1996 edition of the *Subject cataloging manual.* There are few significant changes from edition to edition, but some answers may vary according to the recency of the List you are using.

EXERCISE 1.1

1. Subject: the theme of a work
   Subject heading: a term (word or phrase) that represents the theme of a work

2. There are any number, including:
   Library of Congress Subject Headings
   Sears List of Subject Headings
   MeSH: Medical Subject Headings
   PAIS Thesaurus

EXERCISE 1.2

1. Cataloger:
       Uses headings in subject cataloging
       Maintains consistency within the catalog

2. Reference adviser:
       Uses headings to construct searches when searching the catalog

3. Library user:
       To construct searches in the catalog

4. Acquisitions officer:
       Uses headings to identify subject areas a library might collect in
       Can search a number of sources for items

5. Interlibrary loans officer:
       Uses to help find and/or verify items for loan

6. Author:
       Helps author to use standard or preferred terminology

EXERCISE 1.3

1. Controlled vocabulary:
       Many library catalogs use LCSH, Sears List of Subject Headings
       Medline, PAIS use thesauri
   Uncontrolled vocabulary:
       Full-text databases
       Keyword title searching in catalogs

2. Controlled Vocabulary
    Advantages
    • only one term per concept
    • records hierarchical and associative relations of a concept
    • establishes scope of each topic
    • increases probability that the same term will be used by different catalogs
    • speeds retrieval.

    Disadvantages
    • highly structured
    • may be cumbersome to use
    • user must "learn" the language.

Uncontrolled Vocabulary
    Advantages
    • effort and cost of indexing are reduced
    • process can be automated
    • user can use terms and synonyms requiring no additional knowledge.

    Disadvantages
    • can fail to retrieve all relevant items if all the synonyms are not used
    • may retrieve false hits, e.g., with homonyms.

EXERCISE 1.4

A synonym is a word that has the same meaning as another.

Tools include dictionaries, thesauri.

1.	author	writer
2.	stamp collecting	philately
3.	car	automobile, motor car
4.	monograph	book
5.	trailer	motor home, RV
6.	serial	journal, periodical
7.	hiking	tramping
8.	saturated	soaked
9.	slack	loose, careless
10.	corpulence	bulkiness, obesity
11.	elevators	lifts
12.	hirsute	hairy
13.	shore	beach
14.	rage	anger, party
15.	hemp	marijuana, seaweed

EXERCISE 1.5

A homonym is a word that sounds the same as another, but has a different meaning.

Tools include dictionaries.

1.	slack	1.	loose
		2.	careless
2.	slam	1.	shut with force and noise
		2.	win all tricks (cards) in one deal
3.	toast	1.	bread in slices browned on both sides by heat
		2.	words of congratulations or appreciation spoken before drinking
4.	lag	1.	fall behind
		2.	cover pipes
5.	cuff	1.	trimming on a sleeve
		2.	to strike with open hand

EXERCISE 1.6

1.   d. contain useful or important information

2.   i.   c. not eating properly and not getting enough exercise
      ii. c. the things we must avoid if we are to stay healthy
      iii. c. make resolutions to lead a healthier life
      iv. b. it is better to become a Buddhist
      v.   a. their way of life involved both exercise and relaxation
      vi. Keywords–fitness, relaxation, yoga, diet, exercise, stress
      vii. Because of our unhealthy lifestyle, we need to learn to relax, and yoga and exercise can help.

EXERCISE 2.1

1.   Beverage containers
     Beverage industry
     Beverage processing machinery industry

2.   Beverage containers—Law and legislation
     Beverage containers—Recycling
     Beverage containers—Recycling—Law and legislation
     Beverage industry—Equipment and supplies
     Beverage processing machinery industry—Equipment and supplies

3.   Beverage containers—United States
     Beverage containers—Law and legislation—United States
     Beverage containers—Recycling—Law and legislation—United States
     Beverage industry—United States
     Beverage processing machinery industry—United States

EXERCISE 2.2

1. Craftsmen is not used. Artisans is used.

2. Apprentices is narrower than Artisans.

3. Skilled labor is broader than Artisans.

4. Artisans and Cottage industries are related terms. Both are used.

5. No.

EXERCISE 2.3

	Topic	Correct Heading
1.	Felix the Cat	Felix the Cat (Fictitious character)
2.	Guitar—construction	Correct
3.	Fusion reactors—Fuels	Thermonuclear fuels
4.	Fusion reactors—Australia	Fusion reactors
5.	Semi-conductors	Semiconductors
6.	Guitar and harp music	Correct
7.	Heliophobus plants	Shade-tolerant plants
8.	Seychelles—Coup d'etat, 1977	Seychelles—History—Coup d'etat, 1977
9.	Coup d'etat—Seychelles	Correct
10.	Tempo	Tempo (Computer program language) OR Tempo (Music)

EXERCISE 3.1

1.	The sea	Ocean
2.	Adoption services	Adoption agencies
3.	Adriatic Islands	Islands of the Adriatic
4.	Child actors	Children as actors
5.	Ways of monitoring fetal heart rate	Fetal heart rate monitoring
6.	The impact of jet engine sounds	Jet plane sounds
7.	Oceanic drilling ships in the Atlantic	Deep-sea drilling ships
8.	Catalan political satire	Political satire, Catalan
9.	An introduction to prehistoric agriculture	Agriculture, prehistoric
10.	The wonders of horseradish	Horse-radish

EXERCISE 3.2

1. Morris West's slide collections — Slides (photography)—Private collections
2. Sleep-walking in literature — Sleepwalking
3. Cartoon-makers — Animators
4. Electric converters — Cascade converters
5. Music for harp and guitar — Guitar and harp music
6. Sulky racing — Harness racing
7. Harmony on the keyboard — Keyboard harmony
8. Prehistoric cartography — Cartography, Prehistoric
9. The benefits of asparaginic acid — Aspartic acid
10. Bakery products — Baked products

EXERCISE 4.1

1. Economic conditions in Bologna — Bologna (Italy)—Economic conditions
2. Extensions to buildings — Buildings—Additions
3. Synthesis in organic chemistry — Organic compounds—Synthesis
4. Data processing in credit bureaus — Credit bureaus—Data processing
5. The rights and wages of employees in credit unions — Credit unions—Employees
6. John Brown's raid on Harpers Ferry — Harpers Ferry—History—John Brown's raid, 1859
7. The 1929 depression in Chicago — Depressions—1929—Illinois—Chicago
8. The diagnosis of unipolar depression — Depression, Mental—Diagnosis
9. Renaissance engraving — Engraving, Renaissance
10. Hunting with bows and arrows — Bow-hunting

EXERCISE 4.2

1. Dentistry—Law and legislation — Incorrect — Dentistry—Study and teaching—Law and legislation
2. Paper industry—History — Correct
3. Buildings—Maintenance — Correct
4. Buildings—Maintenance and repair — Allowed, but... — Heading using a free-floating subdivision is allowed, but prefer Buildings—Maintenance, which is included in the list
5. Books—Reviews—Periodicals — Correct
6. Dentistry—Book reviews — Correct

7.	Real property—Finance, personal	Incorrect	Finance, personal only allowed under names of individual persons, and under classes of persons and ethnic groups (See Finance, Public)
8.	Chicago (Ill.)—Appropriations and expenditure	Correct	

EXERCISE 4.3

Banks and banking—Canada
Banks and banking—Canada—Automation
Banks and banking—Canada—Automation—Equipment and supplies
Banks and banking—Canada—Branch banks
Banks and banking—Branch banks—Law and legislation—Canada
Banks and banking—Government ownership—Canada
Banks and banking—Government ownership—Law and legislation—Canada

EXERCISE 4.4

1.	Diseases of the eyelids in China	Eyelids—Diseases—China
2.	Diseases of the forelimbs in Africa	Extremities, Upper—Diseases—Africa
3.	Taxation of show business personalities in Australia	Performing arts—Taxation—Australia
4.	The labeling of bread in Houston	Bread—Labeling—Texas—Houston
5.	The legislation on bread labeling in Oregon	Bread—Labeling—Law and legislation—Oregon
6.	Abnormalities of cattle in Argentina	Cattle—Abnormalities—Argentina
7.	Collective agreements in the airlines in Belgium	Collective labor agreements—Aeronautics—Belgium
8.	Job stress in health professionals in Virginia	Medical personnel—Job stress—Virginia
9.	A report on potato pests in Victoria	Potatoes—Diseases and pests—Australia—Victoria
10.	Historical monuments in Mankato, Minnesota	Monuments—Minnesota—Mankato

EXERCISE 4.5

	Topic	Subject Heading
1.	Parachutes—Testing—Equipment—Certification—United States	Parachutes—Testing equipment—Certification—United States
2.	Scientific apparatus and instruments—Conservation and restoration	Correct
3.	United States—Climate—Measurement	Correct
4.	Birthparents—Identification—Case studies	Correct
5.	Chamber music—Early works to 1800—England	Chamber music—England—Early works to 1800

6.	Murderers—Civil rights—Boston (Mass.)	Correct
7.	Trade-unions—Accounting—Law and Legislation—Michigan	Correct
8.	Tuberculosis vaccines—Maine—Bangor	Correct
9.	Tuberculosis vaccines—Safety regulations—Maine—Bangor	Correct
10.	Separating machinery industry—Corrupt practices—London	Separating machinery industry—England—London—Corrupt practices

EXERCISE 4.6

	Topic	Subject Heading
1.	Bibliography on plant migration	Plants—Migration—Bibliography
2.	Colonization of Zaire	Zaire—Colonization
3.	Pensions of bus drivers in Mexico	Bus drivers—Pensions—Mexico
4.	History of the laws regulating collection agencies in New Zealand	Collection agencies—Law and legislation—New Zealand—History
5.	Satirical cartoons of nurses	Nurses—Caricatures and cartoons
6.	Laboratories for sensory evaluation in Geneva	Sensory evaluation—Switzerland
7.	Diagnosis of mouth cancer in Glasgow	Mouth—Cancer—Scotland—Glasgow—Diagnosis
8.	Testing of instruments used in Atomic absorption spectroscopy in Tokyo	Atomic absorption spectroscopy—Japan—Tokyo—Instruments—Testing
9.	Deterioration of murals in Venice	Mural painting and decoration—Italy—Venice—Deterioration
10.	Care of clothing in the 19th century	Clothing and dress—Care—History—19th century

EXERCISE 5.1

	Topic	Pattern Heading	Heading
1.	The lifecycle of the chipmunk	Fishes	Chipmunk—Life cycles
2.	Longevity of cats	Cattle	Cats—Age
3.	Ellipsis in Albanian	English language	Albanian language—Ellipsis
4.	The psychotropic effects of iodine	Copper	Iodine—Psychotropic effects
5.	Economic conditions of Dutch colonies in Asia	Great Britain—Colonies	Netherlands—Colonies—Asia—Economic conditions
6.	Breeding lions	Cattle	Lions—Breeding
7.	Origins of Zen Buddhism in Japan	Buddhism	Zen Buddhism—Japan—Origin

8.	Anti-lock brake systems for dune buggies	Automobiles	Dune buggies—Anti-lock brake systems
9.	Diagnosing brain abscesses	Foot	Brain—Abscess
10.	Regional variations in the macadamia nut industry	Construction industry Retail trade	Macadamia nut industry—Regional disparities
11.	Production standards of films adapted from Arabic children's stories	English literature	Children's stories, Arabic—Film and television adaption—Production Standards
12.	Research on methods of painting of plastics	Metals Concrete	Plastics—Painting—Research
13.	How French has had an impact on English	English language	French language—Influence on English
14.	Genetic engineering of sheep in New Zealand	Cattle	Sheep—Genetic engineering—New Zealand
15.	How to deal with vapor lock problems in buses	Automobiles	Buses—Fuel systems—Vapor lock—Repairing

EXERCISE 5.2

	Topic	Subject Heading
1.	Liver—Size	Correct
2.	Poets—Exile	Poets—Biography—Exile
3.	Spring wheat—Diseases and pests—Italy —Biological Control	Wheat—Diseases and pests—Biological control—Italy
4.	Sino-French War, 1884-1885—Battles	Chinese-French War, 1884-1885—Campaigns
5.	Guitar—Strings—Materials	Correct
6.	Dogs—Embryos—Canada—Transplantation	Dogs—Embryos—Transplantation—Canada
7.	Llamas—Peru—Handling	Llamas—Handling—Peru
8.	Toes, Dislocation of	Toes—Dislocation
9.	Ranunculus—Time of flowering	Ranunculus—Flowering time
10.	Canola—Disease and pest resistance—Genetic aspects	Correct

EXERCISE 5.3

Topic	Subject Heading
1. Religious aspects of animal experiments from the Islamic viewpoint	Animal experimentation—Religious aspects—Islam
2. Subject headings for astronomy	Subject headings—Astronomy
3. Christian beliefs about salt	Salt—Religious aspects—Christianity
4. German words and phrases in the English language	English language—Foreign words and phrases—German
5. Buddhist aspects of codependency	Codependency—Religious aspects—Buddhism

EXERCISE 6.1

	Topic	Subject Heading
1.	Hyde Park in Tampa, Florida	Hyde Park (Tampa, Fla.)
2.	Isle Royale National Park	Isle Royale National Park (Mich.)
3.	Royal National Park (south of Sydney)	Royal National Park (N.S.W.)
4.	Central Park (in New York)	Central Park (New York, N.Y.)
5.	Statue of Liberty	Statue of Liberty (New York, N.Y.)
6.	Grand Canyon	Grand Canyon (Ariz.)
7.	Brooks Cemetery (in Illinois)	Brooks Cemetery (Homer, Ill.)
8.	Merri River	Merri River (Vic.)
9.	London River (in France)	London River (France and Switzerland)
10.	Amazon River	Amazon River
11.	Death Valley	Death Valley (Calif. and Nev.)
12.	Bond Street (London)	Bond Street (London, England)
13.	17th Street in Washington	Seventeenth Street (Washington, D.C.)
14.	Highway 40 (United States)	United States Highway 40
15.	Hilo Bay	Hilo Bay (Hawaii)
16.	Brooklyn Bridge (in New York)	Brooklyn Bridge (New York, N.Y.)
17.	Westland Park	Westland National Park (N.Z.)
18.	Mount Whitney in California	Whitney, Mount (Calif.)
19.	The Sistine Chapel	Sistine Chapel (Vatican Palace, Vatican City)
20.	Wailing Wall (in Jerusalem)	Western Wall (Jerusalem)

EXERCISE 6.2

	Topic	Subject Heading
1.	American libraries	Libraries—United States
2.	Hospitals in Albuquerque	Hospitals—New Mexico—Albuquerque

96 *LEARN LIBRARY OF CONGRESS SUBJECT ACCESS*

3.	A field guide to birds around Billings in Montana	Birds—Montana—Billings
4.	Animals in southeast Asia	Zoology—Asia, Southeastern
5.	A report on the police in Kentucky	Police—Kentucky
6.	Body surfing on the Gold Coast	Surfing—Australia—Gold Coast (Qld.)
7.	Churches in London, Ontario	Churches—Ontario—London
8.	Parakeets of south-eastern Australia	Australian parakeets—Australia, Southeastern
9.	Art galleries in Kansas City	Art museums—Missouri—Kansas City
10.	Folk songs of Spain	Folkmusic—Spain
11.	Painters from Rocksprings, Wyoming	Painters—Wyoming—Rocksprings
12.	Research into the climate of Anchorage	Climatology—Research—Alaska—Anchorage
13.	Bridges in Rome	Bridges—Italy—Rome
14.	Walking in Richmond, Virginia	Walking—Virginia—Richmond
15.	Education in Vermont	Education—Vermont

EXERCISE 6.3

1. Shakespeare, William, 1616-1664
2. Byatt, A. S. (Antonia Susan), 1936-
3. Hawke, Bob, 1929-
4. Joan, of Arc, Saint, 1412-1431
5. Elizabeth II, Queen of Great Britain, 1926-
6. Tower of London (London, England)
7. Empire State Building (New York, N.Y.)
8. Agar, Agustus, 1890-1986
9. Tyree family
10. Kant, Immanuel, 1724-1804

EXERCISE 6.4

1. Warren, Earl, 1891-1974
2. Bennett, Tony, 1926-
3. Presidents—United States—Biography
4. Pulitzer Prizes—History
5. Taylor family

EXERCISE 7.1

150 o $aAthletics
450 o $aCollege athletics
550 o $aPhysical education and training
550 o $aSports
550 o whaBoxing
550 o whaCollege sports
680 o $isubdivision Athletics under names of individual educational institutions

150 o $aBoxing
450 o $aPrizefighting
550 o wgaAthletics

150 o $aPhysical education and training
550 o $aAthletics

150 o $aSports
550 o $aAthletics

150 o $aCollege sports
550 o wgaAthletics

EXERCISE 8.1

1.   AACRII—Computer assisted instruction

2.   Children, Adopted

3.   Vivisection—History

4.   Daffodils

5.   Artists—Spain

6.   English language—Business English

7.   Car pools—California—San Francisco

8.   Library of Congress—Public relations

9.   Public relations—Libraries

10.   Child health services—Denmark

11.   Musicians—Mexico

12.   Massachusetts—Constitutional law

13.   Cookery, Egyptian

14.   Heraldry
      Crests

15.   Library education—Bibliography

EXERCISE 8.2

1. Rice—Effect of pollution on
2. Photovoltaic power generation
3. Aztecs—Dictionaries and encyclopedias
4. Erotic art
5. Korean War, 1950-1953—Personal narratives, American
6. Sewage—Purification—Biological treatment
7. Flour-mills—Brazil
8. Tramps
9. German language—Dictionaries—Spanish
    Spanish language—Dictionaries—German
10. China—History—1949-1976
11. Architectural drawing
12. Psychokinesis
13. Horn (Musical instrument)—Tuning
14. Piano—Tuning
15. Folk-songs, Eskimo

EXERCISE 8.3

1. Middle Ages—History
2. Columbus (Nebr.)—Telephone directories
3. Begging—History
4. Ship models—Catalogs
5. Hostage negotiations
6. Dogs—Fiction—Bibliography
7. Porcelain—China—Dating
8. Unemployment—Psychological aspects
9. Judaism—Relations—Islam
    Islam—Relations—Judaism
10. Children's poetry
11. Riot control
12. Grail
13. Snakes—Kentucky
14. Single parents
15. Surfing—Hawaii

EXERCISE 8.4

1. Argentina. Armada—Surgeons

2. Pilot Grove Creek (Tex.)

3. Microcomputers

4. Photography of insects

5. Vietnamese Conflict, 1961-1975—Photographs

6. Television—Repairing

7. Public libraries—Services to preschool children

8. Preserved flower pictures

9. Gravity—Measurement

10. Five Precepts (Buddhism)

11. Horsemanship—Officiating

12. Radioactive wastes—Transportation—Law and legislation—Germany

13. Snow and ice climbing—Nepal

14. Widowhood
    Bereavement

15. Waste paper—Recycling

GLOSSARY

AACR2R Anglo-American cataloguing rules second edition 1988 revision. Revision in 1988 of a set of rules for descriptive cataloging developed by the Library Association (Great Britain) and the American Library Association, and published in 1967 in separate British and North American texts; revised into one consolidated text in 1978 (*Anglo-American cataloguing rules second edition–AACR2*). Adopted by major libraries in most English-speaking countries, and translated into many other languages

access point A heading given to a catalog or database record or entry in a bibliography which enables a user to find the item

added entry Any entry, other than the main entry (and subject entries), by which the user can access the catalog, e.g., title, joint author, illustrator, editor, compiler, translator, series, corporate body

author The person chiefly responsible for the intellectual or artistic content of a work, e.g., writer of a book, compiler of a bibliography, composer of a musical work, artist, photographer

authority control The control of access points by establishing and using consistent headings

authority file A collection of authority records containing the preferred forms of headings for names, series and subjects. It can be on cards, microfiche or online

authority record A record of the preferred heading for a person, place, corporate body, series or title and the references to and from the heading

authority work The establishment and maintenance of authority files

authorized heading A term taken from an authorized list of headings and used in a catalog

bibliographic record A catalog entry in card, microtext, machine-readable or other form containing full cataloging information for a given item

biography 1. A written account of a person's life. 2. The branch of literature concerned with people's individual lives

Boolean logic Use of the terms "and", "or", "not" to formulate online search commands, to represent any logical possibility

Boolean operator And: retrieves only items with both terms. Or: retrieves items with either term. Not: retrieves items with one term and not the other. These words are used in the formulation of search strategies for the retrieval of online information

broader term, broader topic BT. A more general subject heading

BT Broader term, broader topic. A more general subject heading

catalog A list of library materials contained in a collection, a library or a group of libraries, arranged according to some definite plan

cataloger A person who prepares catalog entries and maintains a catalog so that library materials can be retrieved efficiently

cataloging The preparation of bibliographic information for catalog records. Cataloging consists of descriptive cataloging, subject cataloging and classification

cataloging-in-publication Cataloging data produced by the national library or other agency of the country of publication, included in the work when it is published

cataloging tools Publications of the international cataloging rules and standards, including *Anglo-American cataloguing rules (AACR), Library of Congress subject headings (LCSH), Library of Congress classification (LCC), Dewey decimal classification (DDC)*

chronological subdivision Also period subdivision. A subdivision which shows the period or span of time covered by a work, or the period in which the work appeared

CIP *See* cataloging-in-publication

classification number Number allocated to a library item to indicate a subject

collocation Arrangement which locates like material together

controlled vocabulary Terms found in an authoritative list of terms, e.g., Library of Congress Subject Headings, a database thesaurus

corporate body An organization or group of people identified by a particular name, and acting as an entity

cross reference *See* reference

database A collection of records in machine-readable format, each record being the required information about one item

descriptor A term used to identify a subject

dictionary catalog A catalog with all the entries arranged in a single alphabetical sequence

direct entry A heading using the specific term which describes the topic, e.g., Creeping fescue

direct subdivision A subdivision which directly follows the main heading or subdivision. Usually used for geographic subdivisions

encyclopedia A systematic summary of all significant knowledge; a summary of the knowledge of one subject. Usually arranged alphabetically

explanatory reference A longer "see" or "see also" reference which explains when a heading or headings should be used

foreword A brief statement of the reasons for the book, usually by the author or editor. It appears after the title page and before the introduction

form 1. The way in which a bibliographic work is arranged, e.g., dictionary. 2. Type of literary work, e.g., poetry, drama

format 1. Appearance and make-up of a book; its size, paper, type, binding, etc. 2. Physical type of an audiovisual item, e.g., slide, filmstrip, etc. 3. Physical organization of a catalog, e.g., card, microfiche, online, etc.

form heading A heading which represents the physical, bibliographic, artistic or literary form of a work, e.g., Encyclopedias and dictionaries, Short stories

form subdivision A subdivision which brings out the form of a work, e.g., —Periodicals, —Bibliography

free-floating subdivision A subdivision which may be used under any existing appropriate LC subject heading

free text vocabulary *See* uncontrolled vocabulary

general reference A reference made to a group of headings, rather than one specific heading, e.g., Dog breeds–*SA names of specific breeds, e.g.,* Bloodhounds, Collies

geographic heading Place name used as a subject heading

geographic name Name of a place–country, state, city, town, suburb, etc.

geographic qualifier The name of a larger geographic entity added to a local place name, e.g., Phoenix (Ariz.)

geographic subdivision Place name used as a subdivision of a topic

hierarchy A system of organization in which narrower topics are part of broader topics

homograph A word which looks the same as another, but has a different meaning

homonym A word which sounds the same as another, and may be spelled the same, but has a different meaning

index 1. An alphabetical list of terms or topics in a work, usually found at the back. 2. A systematically arranged list which indicates the contents of a document or group of documents

indirect entry A heading in which the specific term is a subdivision of a general term, e.g., Ground covers—Lawn grasses—Creeping fescue

indirect subdivision A subdivision in which another element is interposed between the main heading and the specific subdivision. Usually used for geographic subdivisions

initial article The word which introduces a noun at the beginning of a title, e.g., the, a, an

inverted heading A heading in which the normal order of the words is reversed, in order to group like terms together in the subject list, e.g., Cookery, French

journal A periodical issued by an institution, corporation or learned society containing current information and reports of activities or works in a particular field

jurisdictional heading A geographic heading used for a political jurisdiction, that is the name of an area used to represent a government

keyword A significant term found in a document which identifies subject content

Library of Congress The library of the United States Congress; the de facto national library of the United States

Library of Congress Subject Headings The authoritative list of subject headings compiled and maintained by the Library of Congress

literary warrant The volume of books written, or likely to be written, on a topic

monograph A publication either complete in one part or in a finite number of separate parts

multiple subdivision A subdivision which is used to show the creation of similar subdivisions under the same heading - e.g., Ocean currents—subdivided by body of water, e.g., Ocean currents—Atlantic Ocean

name authority file A collection of authority records containing the preferred forms of headings for names, including personal and corporate names. It can be on cards, microfiche or online

narrower term, narrower topic NT. A more specific subject heading

natural language Also free text vocabulary, uncontrolled vocabulary. Terms taken directly from the work, without reference to a list of subject headings, thesaurus or authority file

non-jurisdictional heading A geographic heading used for a place other than a political jurisdiction, e.g., Great Barrier Reef, Golden Gate Bridge

non-preferred term *See* unauthorized heading

NT Narrower term, narrower topic. A more specific subject heading

other title information Also subtitle. Title on an item other than the title proper or parallel or series title; also any phrase appearing in conjunction with the title proper

pattern heading A heading which serves as a model of subdivisions for headings in the same category, e.g., the pattern of subdivisions for "Foot" can be followed for any similar part of the body

periodical A serial with a distinctive title intended to appear in successive parts at stated and regular intervals. Often used as a synonym for serial

period subdivision *See* chronological subdivision

phrase heading A heading consisting of a group of words

post-coordinate Of subject headings or other search terms, put together by the user at the time of searching. Refers to terms used for searching an online index or database, where the computer combines the terms to carry out the search

pre-coordinate Of subject headings or other search terms, put together by the cataloger or indexer

preface The author's or editor's reasons for the book. It appears after the title page and before the introduction

preferred term Also authorized heading. A term taken from an authorized list of headings and used in a catalog

qualifier An addition to a name, etc., enclosed in parentheses

reference A direction from one heading to another

related term, related topic RT. A subject heading at the same level of specificity to another heading and related in subject matter

retrospective conversion Changing older records, usually into machine-readable form

RT Related term, related topic. A subject heading at the same level of specificity to another heading and related in subject matter

SA See also. A direction from one heading to another when both are used

scan 1. To examine every item in a collection to determine usefulness for information retrieval. 2. To read a printed document into a computer

scope note A note describing the range and meaning of a subject heading

search strategy 1. The approach adopted to finding information on a particular topic. 2. The search statements used to answer an enquiry

search term A word, phrase or number entered by a user to find the records on a database which match the term

see also reference A direction from one heading to another when both are used

see reference Also USE reference. A direction from one heading which is not used to another heading which is used

serial A publication issued in successive parts and intended to be continued indefinitely

specific reference A reference from one heading to another

subdivision An extension of a subject heading which indicates an aspect—form, topic, place or period

subject analysis Identification of the intellectual content of a work

subject authority file A file of all the subject headings used in the catalog, and the relevant references

subject authority record A record of a subject heading which shows the preferred form, the authority used to determine the heading and the references to and from the heading in the catalog

subject cataloging Describing the content of a work using subject headings

subject entry An entry under the heading for the subject

subject heading A heading which describes a subject and provides subject access to a catalog

subordinate body A corporate body which is part of a larger corporate body

subtitle *See* other title information

summary The essential points of an article or literary work

synonym A word with the same meaning as another

thesaurus 1. A work containing synonymous and related words and phrases. 2. A list of controlled terms used in a database

title A word or phrase which names the item

title proper The main name of an item, including alternative title(s) but excluding parallel titles and other title information

topical heading A heading which represents a subject or topic

topical subdivision A subdivision which represents an aspect of the main subject other than form, period or place

UF Used for. The notation used with a preferred heading, which shows the non-preferred heading so that a *see* reference can be made, e.g., "Capture at sea - UF Maritime capture" means that "Capture at sea" is the preferred heading, not "Maritime capture"

unauthorized heading Also non-preferred term. A term which is not taken from an authorized list of headings and should not be used

uncontrolled vocabulary Terms taken directly from the work, without reference to a list of subject headings, thesaurus or authority file

used for reference UF. The notation used with a preferred heading, which shows the non-preferred heading so that a *see* reference can be made, e.g., "Capture at sea - UF Maritime capture" means that "Capture at sea" is the preferred heading, not "Maritime capture"

USE reference Also see reference. A direction from one heading which is not used to another heading which is used

vocabulary control Restriction of the terms in a catalog, bibliography or index to those taken from a list of subject headings or thesaurus

BIBLIOGRAPHY

Aluri, Rao, D., Alasdair Kemp, and John J. Boll, *Subject analysis in online catalogs,* Englewood, Colo., Libraries Unlimited, 1991.

Chan, Lois Mai, *Library of Congress subject headings: principles and application* 3rd ed., Englewood, Colo., Libraries Unlimited, 1995.

Langridge, D. W., *Subject analysis: principles and procedures*, London, Bowker-Saur, 1989.

Library of Congress, *Cataloging service bulletin,* Washington, D.C., Library of Congress, 1978-

Library of Congress, *Free-floating subdivisions: an alphabetical index,* Washington, D.C., Library of Congress, 1989-

Library of Congress, *Library of Congress subject headings,* various editions, Washington, D.C., Library of Congress.

Library of Congress, *Subject cataloging manual: subject headings* 5th ed., Washington, D.C., Library of Congress, 1996.

INDEX

authority
   control, 56
   files, 56-67
   records, 56-67
   work, 56-67
biography, 52-54
broader terms, *see* BT
BT, 23, 26, 57-59
cataloging-in-publication, 13
chronological subdivisions, 32
controlled vocabulary, 7
cross references, *see* references
direct headings, 16
direct subdivisions, 39
form headings, 29
form subdivisions, 31
free-floating subdivisions, 33, 68-74
free text vocabulary, *see* uncontrolled
   vocabulary
geographic
   names, 47-50
   qualifiers, 49, 50-51
   subdivisions, 32, 34, 36
hierarchy, 27
homonyms, 10
indirect headings, 36
jurisdictional headings, 48
Library of Congress Subject Headings,
   18-55
multiple subdivisions, 45
name authority files, 47, 56
names, 47-55
   see also geographic names, personal
   names
narrower terms, *see* NT

natural language, *see* uncontrolled
   vocabulary
non-jurisdictional headings, 49
NT, 23, 26, 57-59
pattern headings, 40-43, 75-86
period subdivisions, *see* chronological
   subdivisions
personal names, 52-55
post-coordination, 9
pre-coordination, 9
qualifiers, 50-51
references, 22-25
related terms, *see* RT
RT, 23, 26, 57-59
SA, 23, 26-27, 57
scope notes, 20
see also references, *see* SA
see references, *see* USE
subdivisions, 31-39, 40-46
   see also chronological subdivisions, form
   subdivisions, free-floating subdivisions,
   geographic subdivisions, multiple
   subdivisions, topical subdivisions
subject analysis, 11-16
subject authorities, 56-63
subject headings lists, 6-7
synonyms, 9
terminology, 16
thesaurus, 7
topical headings, 19, 29
topical subdivisions, 31
UF, 22
uncontrolled vocabulary, 8
USE, 22, 26-27
vocabulary control, 7

ABOUT THE AUTHOR

Jacki Ganendran is an experienced cataloger and library educator who has taught the use of Library of Congress subject headings for many years. She has been course coordinator of the Library Studies Program and is currently Head of Computing and Information Management at the Canberra Institute of Technology in Australia.

DEMCO